HAL•LEONARD®

# BANJO PLAY-ALONG

AUDIO ACCESS INCLUDED

# CELTIC BLUEGRASS

Arranged and recorded by Mike Schmidt
Recording credits:
Mike Schmidt – Banjo, Guitar, Bass
Bruce King – Mandolin
Paul Kienitz – Fiddle

**PLAYBACK+**
Speed • Pitch • Balance • Loop

To access audio visit:
**www.halleonard.com/mylibrary**

Enter Code
4546-9583-7343-9077

ISBN 978-1-4950-6398-5

HAL•LEONARD®
7777 W. BLUEMOUND RD. P.O. BOX 13819 MILWAUKEE, WI 53213

In Australia Contact:
**Hal Leonard Australia Pty. Ltd.**
4 Lentara Court
Cheltenham, Victoria, 3192 Australia
Email: ausadmin@halleonard.com.au

Visit Hal Leonard Online at
**www.halleonard.com**

# Performance Notes
**By Mike Schmidt**

Thank you for purchasing *Celtic Bluegrass*. This is a collection of play-along tunes intended for the intermediate to advanced player of the five-string Bluegrass banjo.

The tunes in this book are presented in several different keys. Because a capo is used, they're still written and played in a standard G tuning. So, for example, a tune in the key of A is capoed on the second fret and still thought of and played in terms of G. In this book, for the most part, the key of D is capoed on the second fret and played in terms of C. Because of the style, there are lots of open strings required, so with a capo, the banjo player can pretty much think in terms of the familiar keys of G and C. Of course there are exceptions, but this covers a lot of the music we play, and all the tunes in this book. That said, remember that the performance notes make references to G and C position, even though we might be in another key. Knowing the chord numbers is good, too. You know, the I, IV, and V symbols. Above the staves, the chords are shown two ways. For the banjo, the chord symbols in parentheses show what *you're* playing, and the chords directly above are the actual chords played by accompanists, in the true key. Bass, mandolin, and fiddle don't use capos, so this is for them.

Just because you see a given chord does not mean you, the banjo (or other solo instrument) player, should automatically put that chord position down on the fretboard. You're playing the melody, and often play single notes through those chords. There are times when you will, particularly when you're playing backup chops), but it's not a given in lead parts. Please keep this in mind.

An important part of learning any instrument is playing with others. This is important at any ability level. This book and accompanying audio are the answer. Each tune has two corresponding audio tracks: one with the full band so you can hear the banjo parts, and one without the banjo, so you can play along with the rest of the band. Because it's recorded, the band won't stop if you make a mistake. This trains you to keep going no matter what happens, just like you'd do in a performance. The band isn't going to stop, so pretend it never happened and just keep going. This is a valuable ability.

Another thing to consider here is the rhythm and speed at which the banjo is being played. This is an intermediate to advanced-level book, but the recorded tunes are still a bit slower than you might ultimately play them. With that comes an occasional, involuntary change to the rhythm of the notes. As written, you are looking at mostly eighth notes; as played, these all have equal value. This is true for medium and fast tempo tunes, but if you listen to a slower tune, you might notice that the player will tend to "swing" the note values slightly. By "swing," we mean that each pair of notes is played with a bit of a stagger. The first of the two is of slightly longer duration while the second is slightly shorter. If you read music, you might think of it as if each pair of notes is a dotted eighth and a 16th note. It's easier to listen to the recording and feel it than to explain it in writing. Someone once said, "Talking about music is like dancing about architecture." I think that applies here. Listen to the recording for "The Red Haired Boy." That should explain it much better than I can here.

With the exception of "Billy in the Low Ground," every tune in this book has two banjo parts, or "breaks." The first banjo break is a bit easier and the second is a bit more challenging. When playing along with the recording, remember that you can substitute the first break for the second. The chords are the same, so as soon as you know the first break, you can start practicing with the recording. The backup chords are provided for the other instrumental breaks, too!

## Backup
As mentioned, we also address basic backup techniques in these arrangements. While not intended as a lesson book, this still warrants discussion. Since there are typically no percussion instruments in a Bluegrass band, other

instruments can, and do, take these roles. It depends on the band, but you'll often find the banjo and mandolin taking on the role of the snare drum when they're not taking a break, as you will hear in the play-along audio. During their lead breaks, both the banjo and mandolin are playing lots of rapid-fire notes, usually two notes to each beat. When one of these instruments is playing a solo, the other can play upbeats, not only to give that backbeat rhythm, but literally to get out of the soloist's way. Some banjo players choose to continue playing rolls behind a lead mandolin part, but in my opinion, that can get cluttered and can distract from the lead player. In the play-along audio, when one instrument is playing a lead break, the other is playing the backbeat accompaniment. Believe me, as a banjo player, the other players will appreciate it if you choose to do upbeats rather than continuing to do rolls. You will see that, while I write the backup parts here as upbeat chops, I occasionally throw in a tag lick at the end of a phrase, but still it's minimal.

There are three positions for a major chord on the banjo: a barre chord, a D-position, and an F-position. This means you use the shape of a D or F chord, but on different frets to make different chords. A barre is simply putting one finger across all the strings on the same fret.

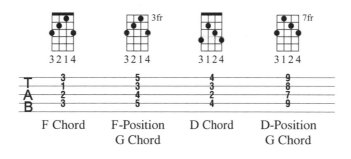

| F Chord | F-Position<br>G Chord | D Chord | D-Position<br>G Chord |

So, start by playing an F chord. If you move this up two frets, keeping the same finger position, it will become a G chord. A barre across the 5th fret is C, and on the 7th fret is D.

The backup parts written in this book are not etched in stone; they're suggestions. As long as you play the right chords, you're free to do anything you like. For example, if what's written alternates between two inversions (positions) of a given chord, stay in one of those positions if it's more comfortable for you. If the book shows a bit of a tag lick at the end of a phrase and you'd rather play chops, go for it.

**"Billy in the Low Ground"**
This is one of two tunes in this book that traditionally uses only fiddle and banjo. For that reason, we've departed from the usual format. Instead of two banjo breaks with another instrument in the middle, the banjo pretty much plays rolls throughout to complement the fiddle. So while the fiddle plays the first break, the banjo is right there with a counter melody. Earlier, I mentioned that I usually play upbeats on the banjo behind the lead instrument. This works fine, but with a fiddle playing longer notes, the banjo can play more rolls without it getting too busy or cluttered as it might with a mando or guitar solo.

The second break is more banjo-centered while the fiddle backs off a bit, and finally, the last break is a duet between the two.

We added a bass part to the recording to help keep you keep the beat while playing with the "play-along" audio.

**"Cluck Old Hen"**

Here, we have a modal sort of tune, going between the I and VII chords quite a bit. I like that sound, but there are a few challenges. Beginning with the first two measures, the second half of each is similar, but different enough that you may have to go over it a few times. Be careful to start the second measure with the pick-hand index finger. Because it's a third-string note, it's tempting to use your thumb, but you just used you thumb to pick the previous note, so it's much smoother to use your index finger.

In Section B, starting at measure 9, notice the difference in timing between the slides and the hammer-ons. The slides are the typical pair of 16th notes, while the hammer-ons are just eighth notes, so don't rush those. They're exactly the same speed as if they were picked.

At the end of each break, there is a one-beat measure. It's labeled with a 2/4 time signature, which normally equates to two beats. But in this instance, the measure is only one beat since this tune is written in cut time, and half notes set the pulse. It first happens at measure 16, and again at measures 34 and 52.

In Section F, starting at measure 45, the "clucking" sound is made by simply muting the strings with the left hand. I pick with just the middle finger, but if you use both middle and index, you can get a fatter sound; it's something to experiment with. This section has the same type of hammer-ons discussed in Section B above.

**"Devil's Dream"**

"Devil's Dream" is in the key of D. For this one, I capo on the 7th fret and play in a G-position. This is a great fiddle tune, and the banjo plays a melodic style throughout. Melodic style is a scale-wise or step-wise approach, allowing a more specific melody to be played. This works great for fiddle tunes, particularly if you're playing in unison. While it sometimes *sounds* complicated, it can be surprisingly easy to play. For example, in measures 3 and 4, it's just a chord position held down while picking a specific string sequence.

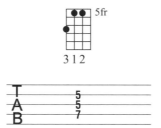

On the other hand, measures 7 and 8 require movement in the left hand that may need some practice. Still, it sounds great.

The first half of the second banjo break is similar to that of the first break, but the second half is a pleasing variation on the chorus. This takes place in measures 57 through 65.

**"Fisher's Hornpipe"**

This is another tune in D, but with a difference. The first break is capoed on the 2nd fret and played in a C-position in a standard Scruggs style, but for the second banjo break, the capo is moved up to the 7th fret and it's played in a G-position in a more melodic style. We're not saying that you *have* to change your capo and play both these breaks as presented here; we just wanted to offer some choices. If you play this with a band, changing the capo with the required tuning adjustments may not be practical; you'd have to do it during someone else's break. But in the comfort of your practice room, you have the luxury of a pause button. For the recording, we kept the banjo capoed on the second fret for the backup to the mandolin and didn't change until the second banjo break.

At the end of measure 20, notice what should be the V chord. The last note is a fretted 3 on the first string. This is the beginning of a move to the F-position chord (IV) immediately following. It's not an intentional anticipation, but it works like one. In reality, it's a tad easier than getting the whole chord down at once at the beginning of the next measure. This happens again at the end of measure 54. The D-position chord switches to an F-position, and the pinky gets there (on the 10th fret) just a fraction before the rest of the chord. You don't have to do this. If you're fast enough to finish that measure with the 7th fret instead of making the move, please do so.

When playing along, note that the mandolin is playing *downbeats* in the first four measures of the tune, then switches to the more typical upbeats. Don't let this throw you.

### "Little Maggie"

"Little Maggie" is a bit different in several ways. First of all, we've done double breaks here, rather than the usual single breaks. It seems this is a tune that usually calls for a double break. I've found in my experience that I'll get through it, and just as I think I'm finishing up, someone yells out, "Do it again!" So, rather than be surprised anymore, I just prepare for a double break. Section A is once through, Section B is the second time. In the mandolin break, Sections C and D are the two times through, and in the second banjo break, it's Sections E and F.

Another difference is in the second banjo break. Notice that (speaking in terms of G), in the first banjo break and the mandolin break, the progression does two measures of G (I), two measures of F (VII), and then back to G (I). In the second banjo break, instead of the two measures of F, we have one of F and one of D (V)! This happens at measures 68, 76, 84, and 92. I find that some performers like it one way, and some like it the other, so I thought it would be good to show both. Always remember that you can do it either way – or both ways, for that matter; it doesn't have to be like we did it here.

Watch for a particular rhythmic detail in measures 86 and 87. The hammer-ons in measure 86 are straight eighth notes and not the usual pair of 16ths and an eighth. These are hammered at the same speed they would be if picked, not snuck in between two picked notes. In measure 87, there's one more of these slow hammer-ons, then a quick combination of a hammer-on and a pull-off. Listen to the recording; this happens at about 1:39. Similar slow eighth-note hammer-ons appear in measures 4, 12, 20, and 28.

### "Over the Waterfall"

In this arrangement, we combine Scruggs style and melodic playing. It's challenging but a lot of fun. The first thing to notice is that this tune is in the key of D… in G position. That means it's capoed on the 7th fret! Doug Dillard did this in several tunes, and personally, I like the sound of the banjo capoed this high.

Like "Billy in the Low Ground," we've added a bass part; when you're practicing the "play-along" version, it will help you keep a steady beat.

### "The Red Haired Boy"

Another combination of Scruggs style and melodic. Both banjo breaks switch freely between the styles, making it a very cool tune to play.

In the first half of the chorus of the second banjo break (Section F), the rest of the band plays drones on the D (I) chord; in the second half, the band resumes the regular progression. You can play every break like this or just the last one. Your choice.

In the second banjo break, specifically measure 62, there's a series of pull-offs out of an F-position. The first half of the measure uses a pull-off on the second string, while the second half pulls off on the third. After the first pull-off (2nd string), be sure to put the index finger back down, because you're still in that F-position and need it to be fretted properly.

**"Soldier's Joy"**
Once again, we're in the key of D, capoed on the 7th fret, and playing one Scruggs style break and one melodic break. The styles are mixed a bit within each break, however.

Notice in the Section B, the chorus of the first break, there's a slight variation on the repeat. In measures 17 through 19, it's pretty much straight quarter notes; but in measures 25 through 27, while basically the same thing, there are some hammer-ons in there just to spruce it up a bit.

# Billy in the Low Ground

**Traditional**

G tuning:
(5th-1st) G-D-G-B-D

**Key of C**
Capo V

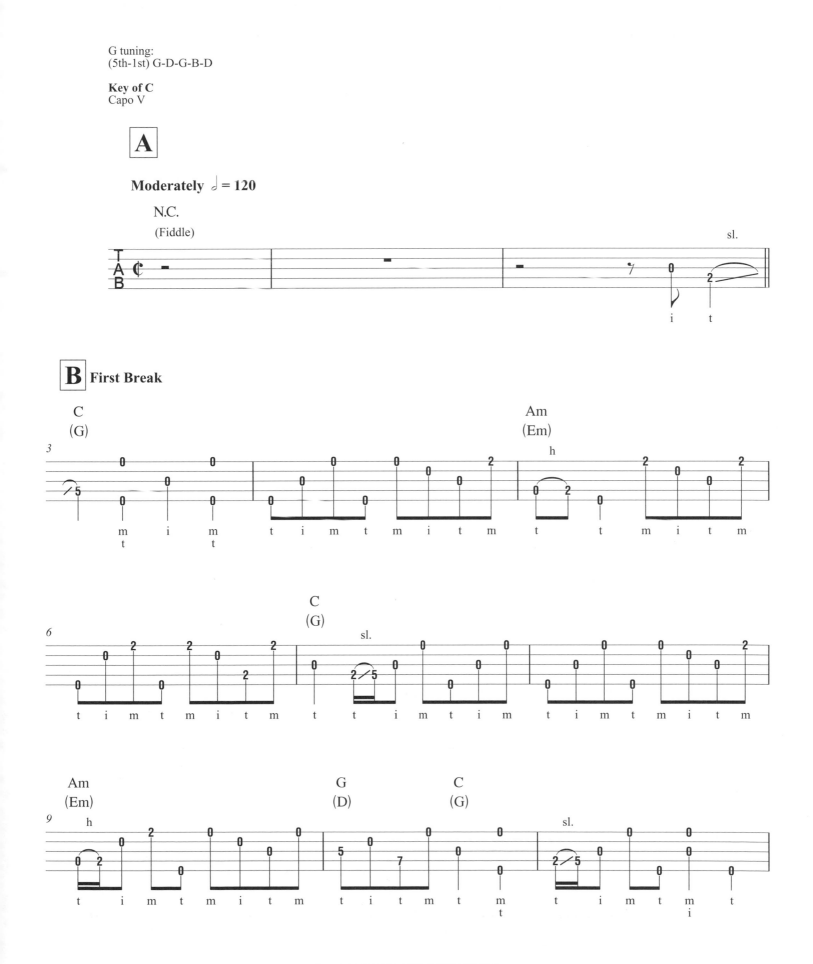

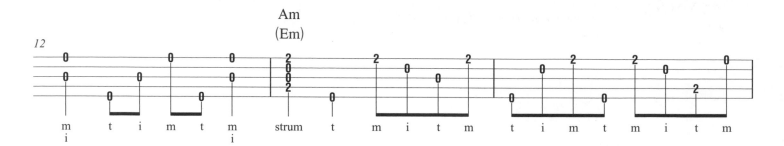

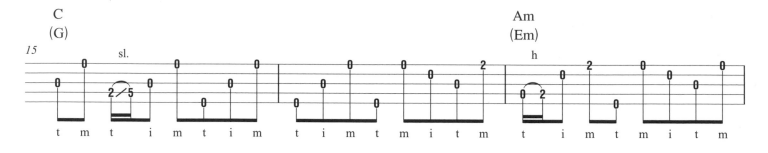

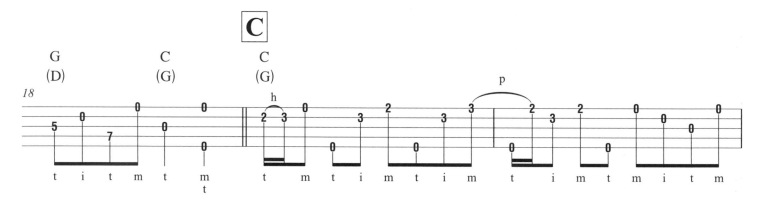

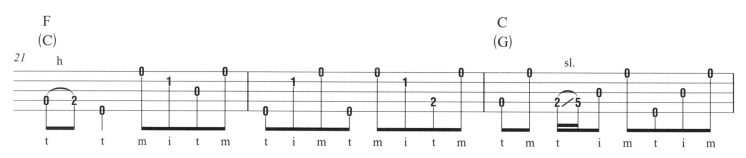

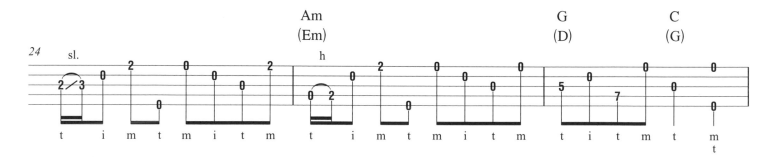

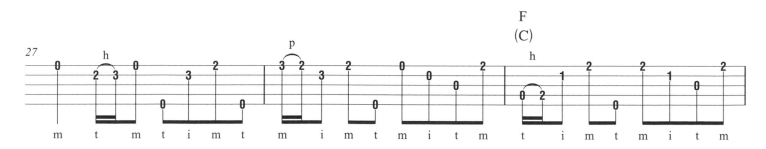

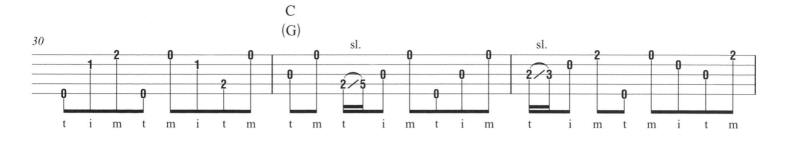

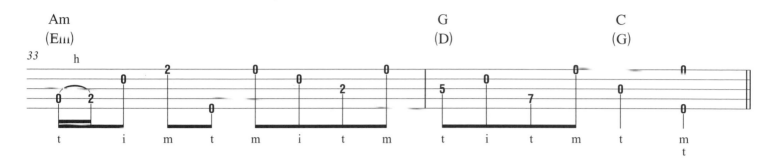

## D 2nd Break

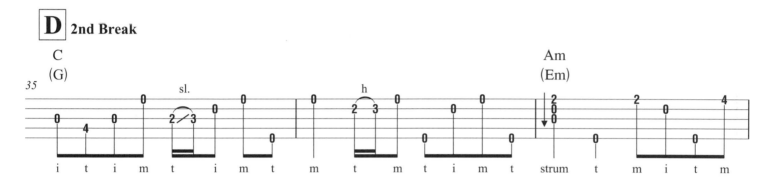

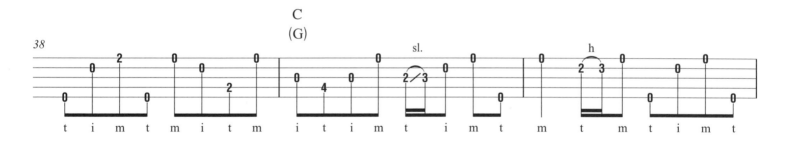

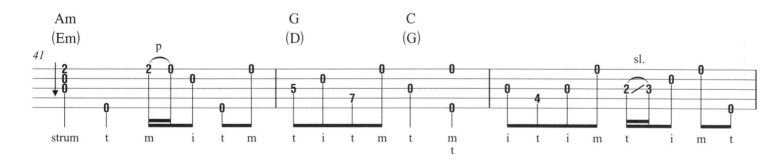

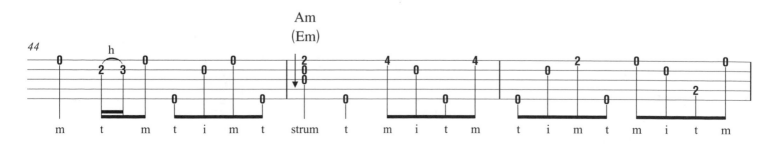

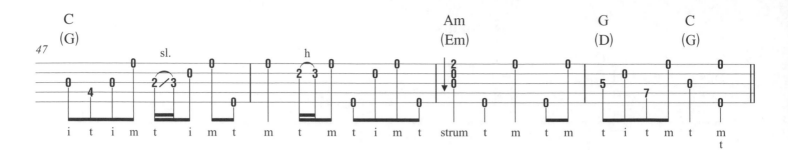

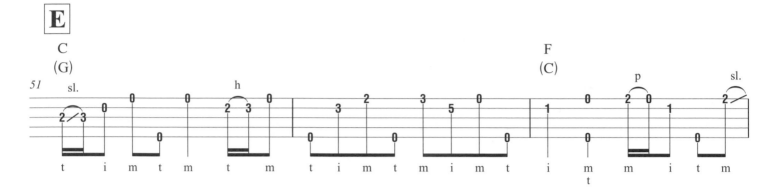

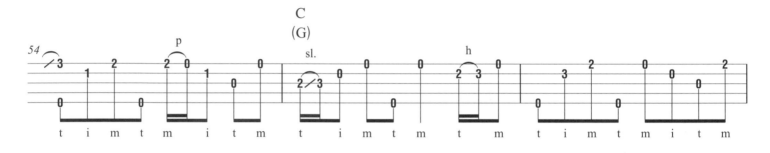

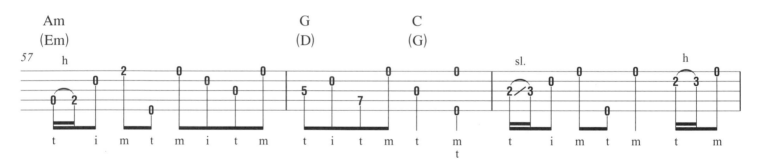

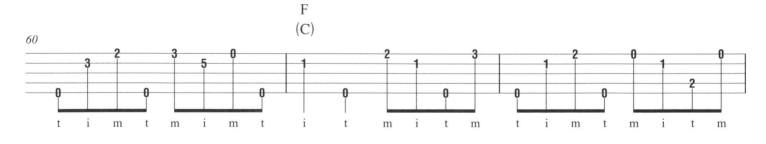

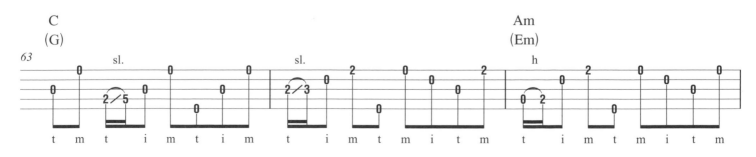

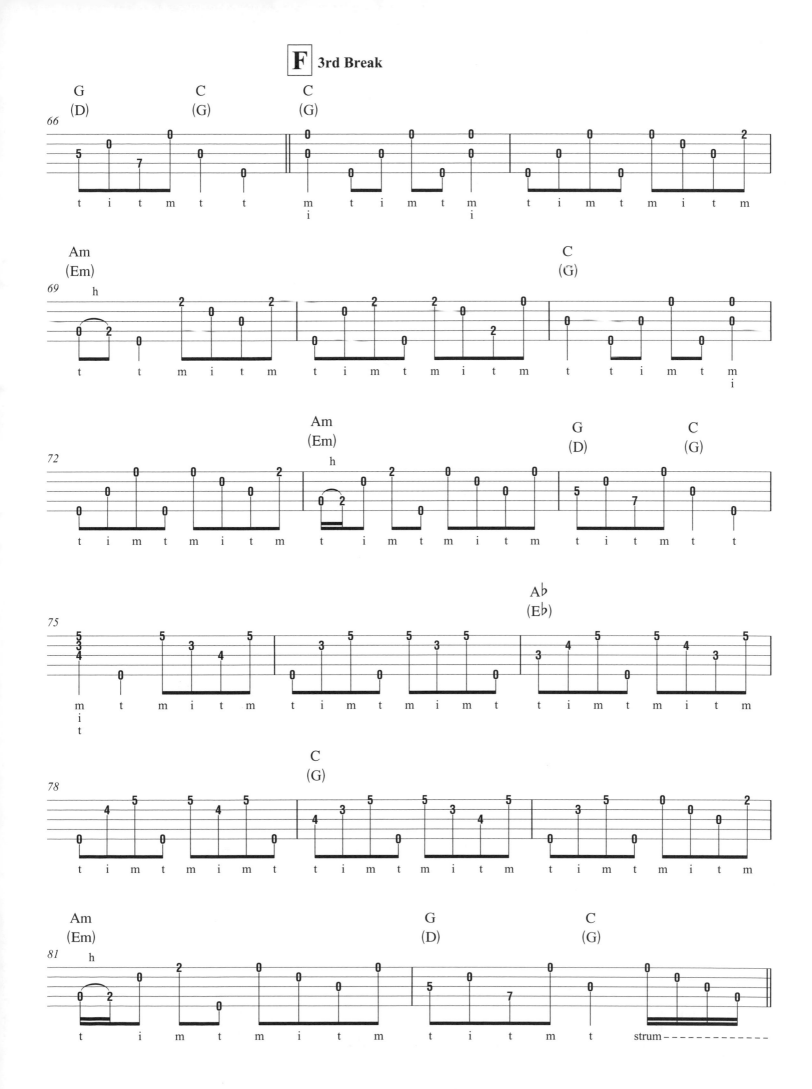

**F** 3rd Break

11

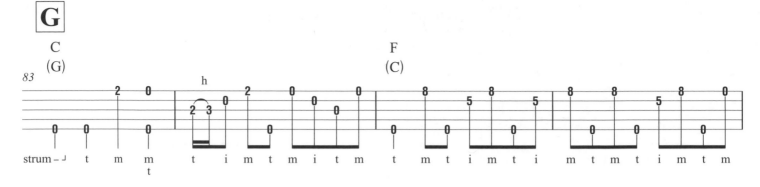

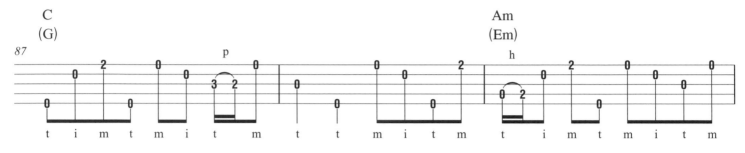

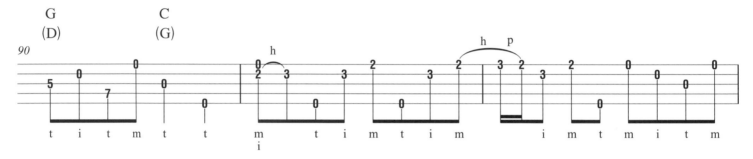

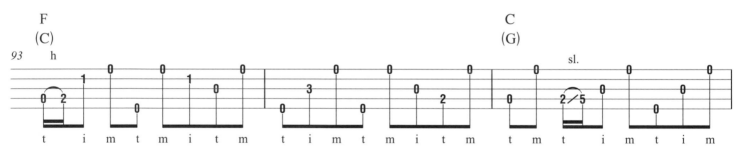

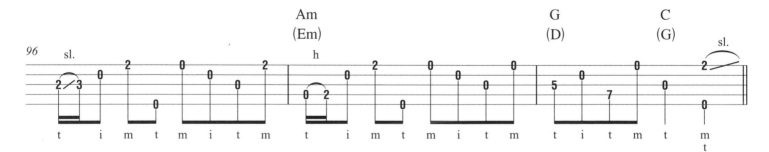

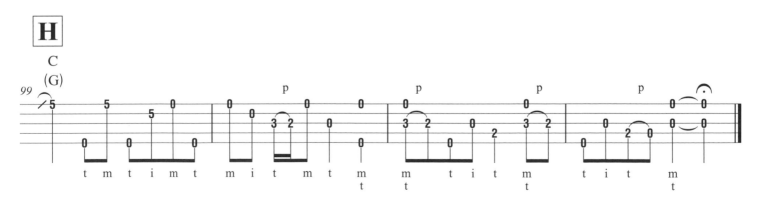

# Cluck Old Hen

**Traditional**

G tuning:
(5th-1st) G-D-G-B-D

**Key of A**
Capo II

 **Banjo Break**

**Moderately slow** ♩ = 96

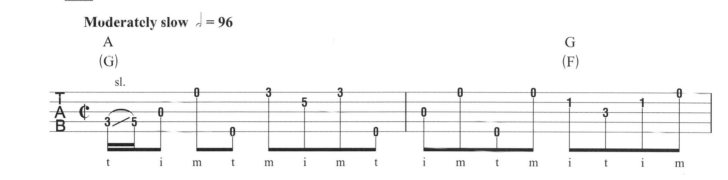

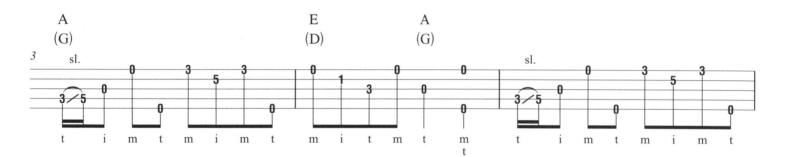

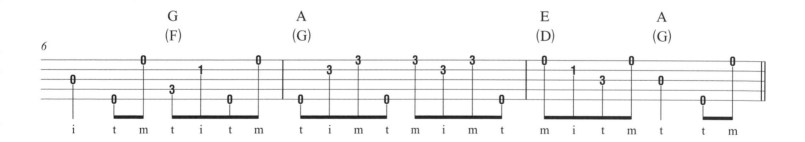

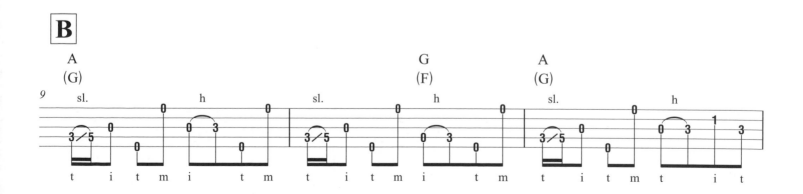

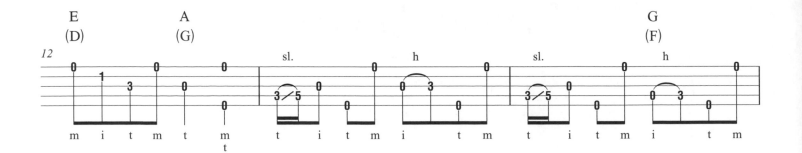

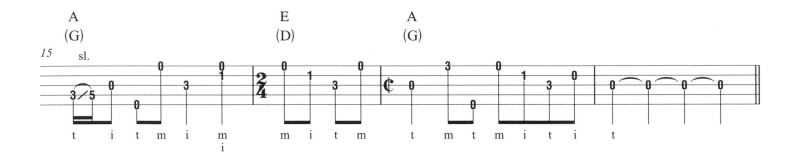

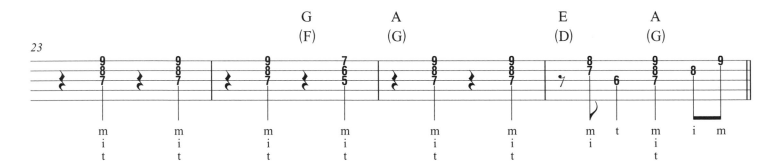

**C** Mandolin Break

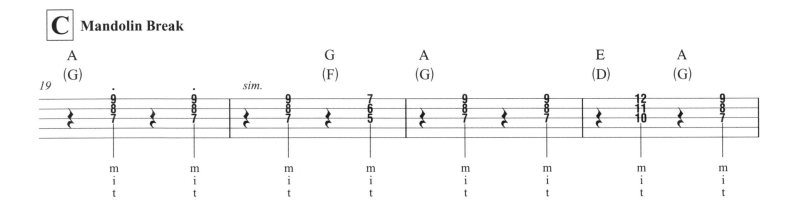

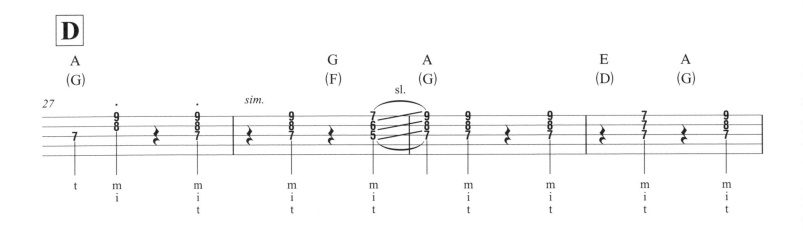

**D**

14

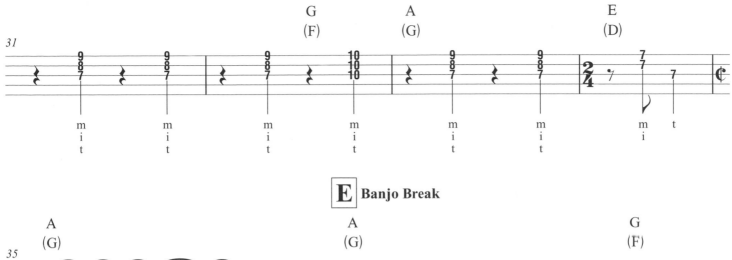

**E** Banjo Break

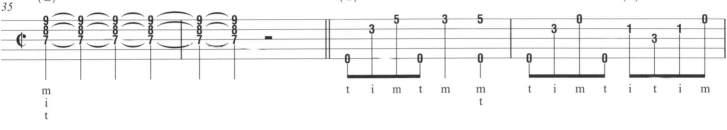

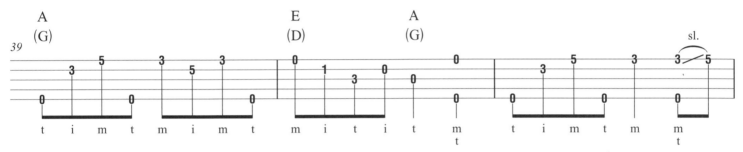

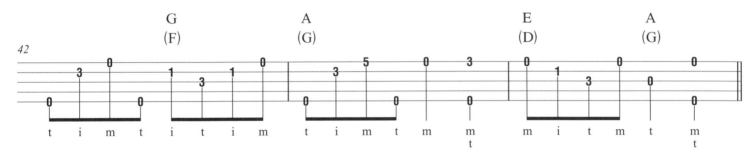

**F**

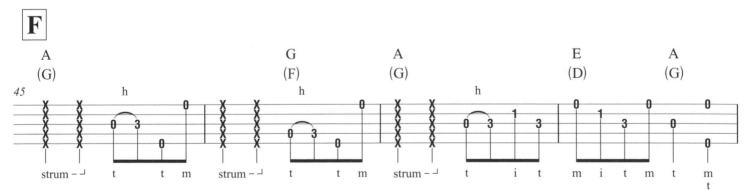

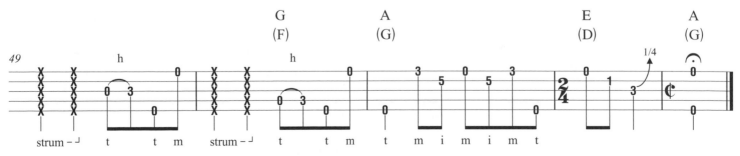

# Devil's Dream

**Traditional**

G tuning:
(5th-1st) G-D-G-B-D

**Key of D**
Capo VII

**A** Banjo Break

Moderately ♩ = 104

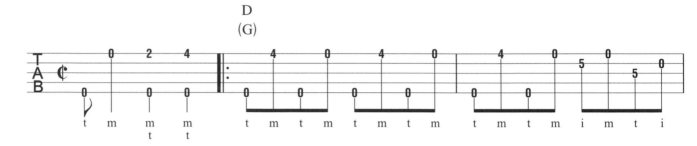

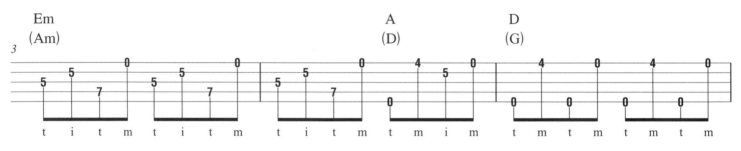

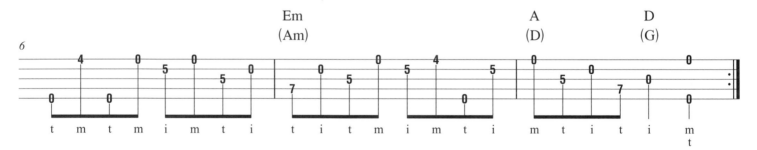

**B**

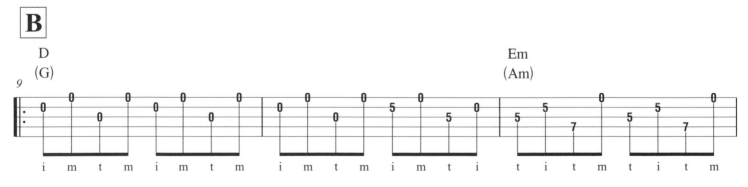

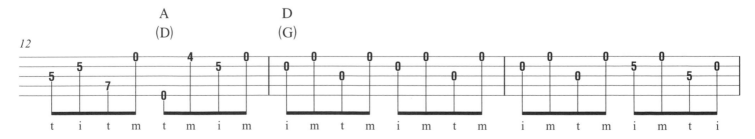

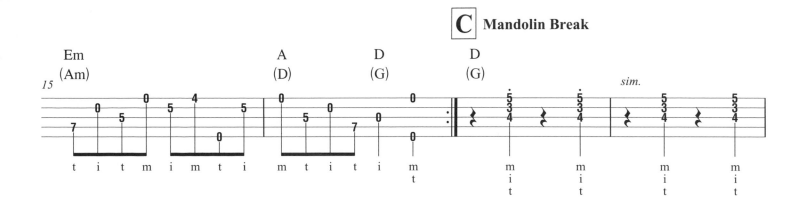

C Mandolin Break

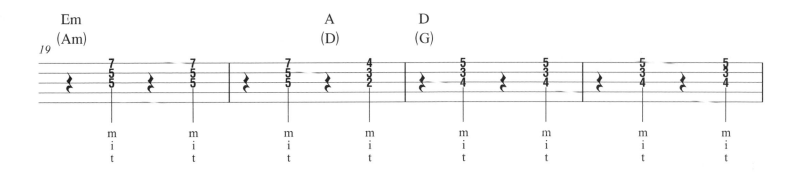

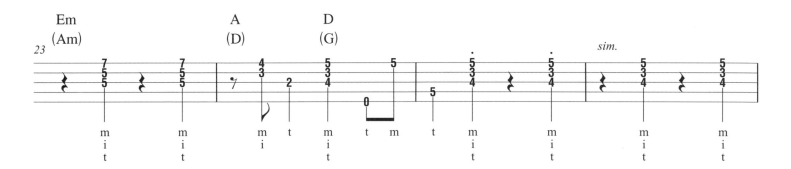

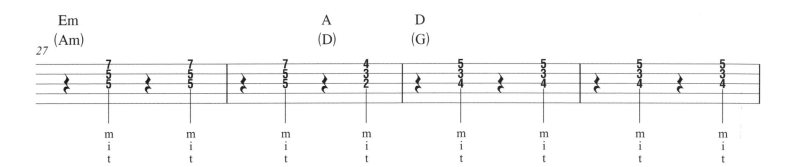

D

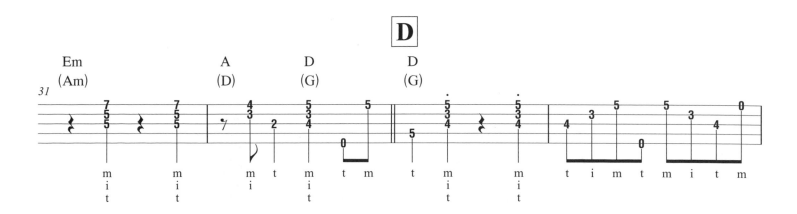

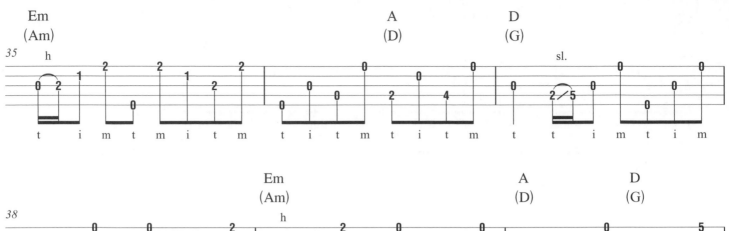

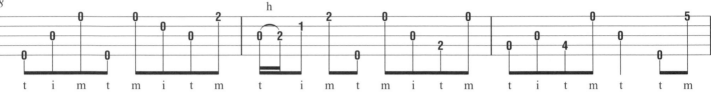

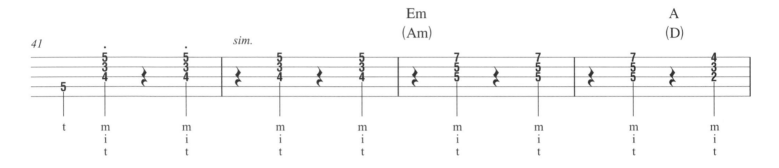

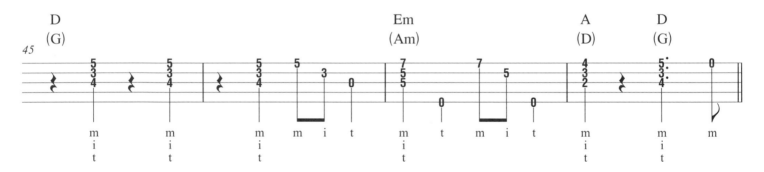

**E** **Banjo Break**

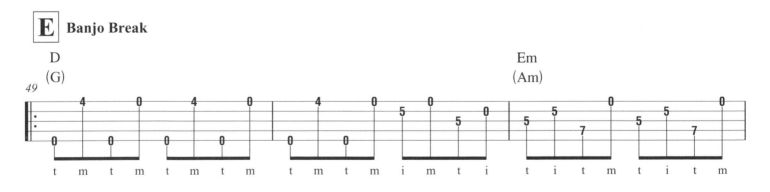

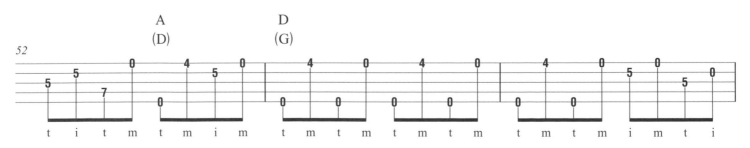

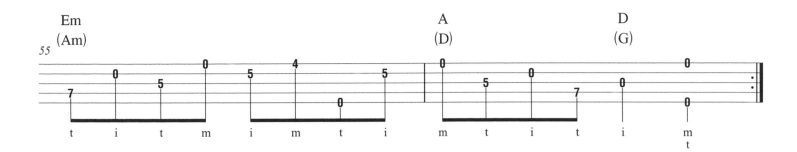

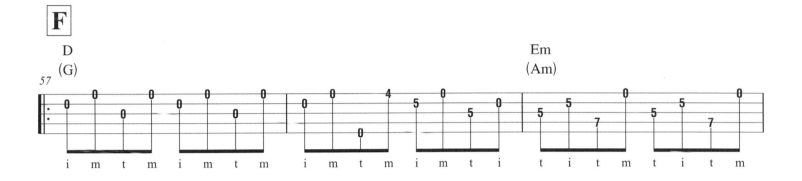

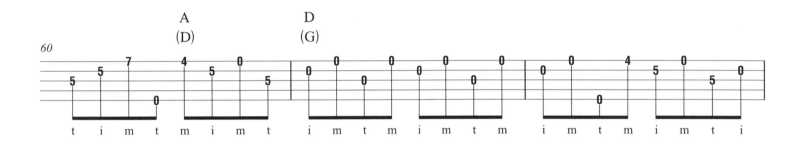

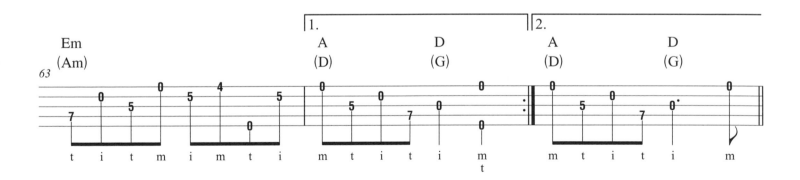

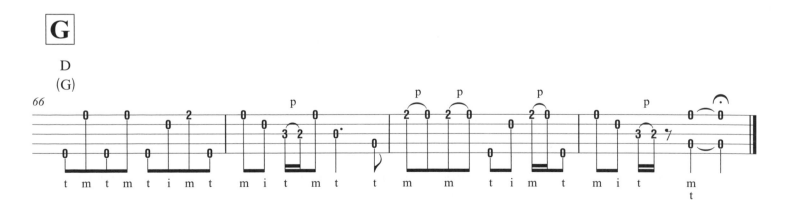

# Fisher's Hornpipe

**Traditional**

G tuning:
(5th-1st) G-D-G-B-D

**Key of D**
Capo II

**A** Banjo Break

Moderately slow ♩ = 96

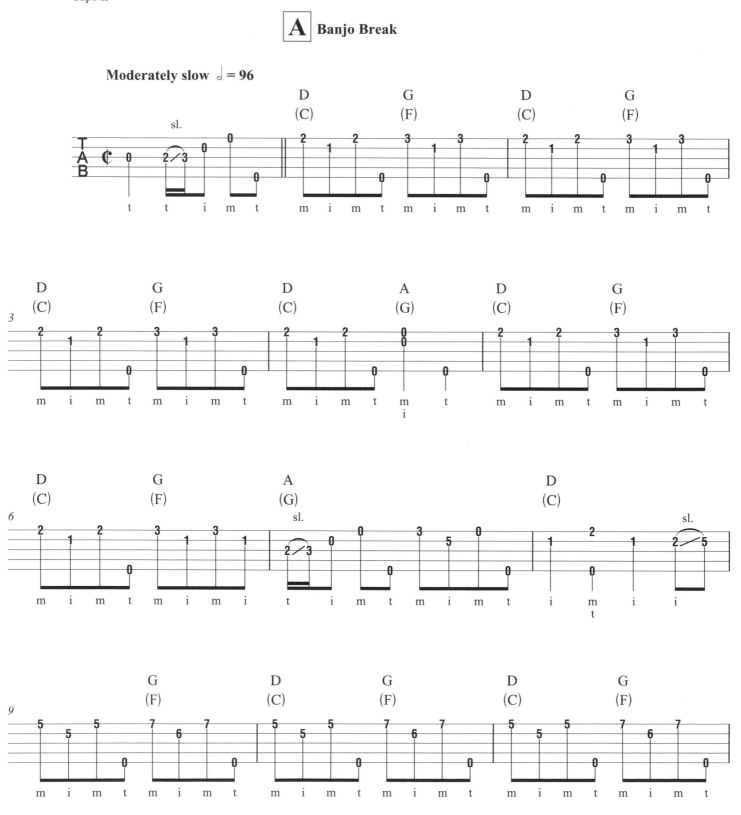

Copyright © 2017 by HAL LEONARD LLC
International Copyright Secured   All Rights Reserved

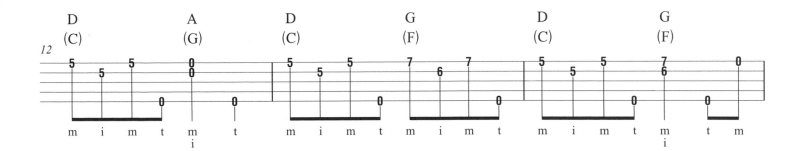

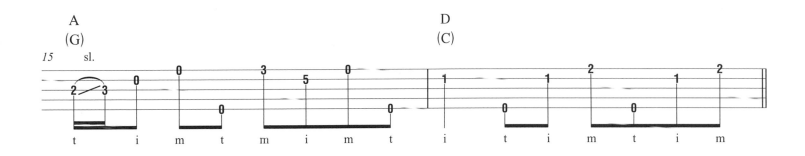

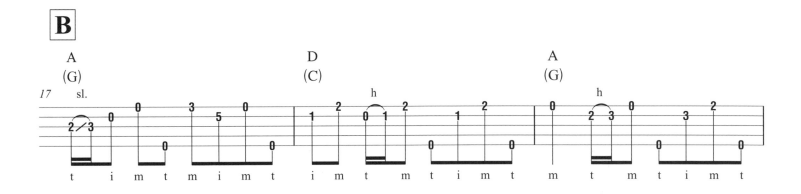

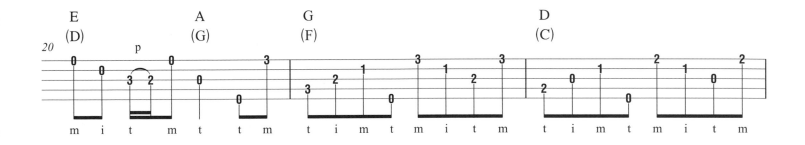

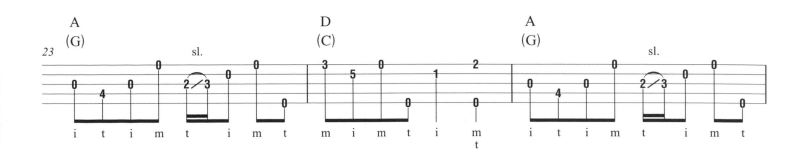

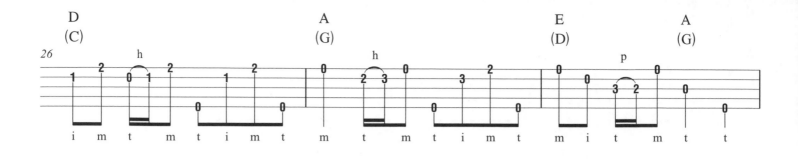

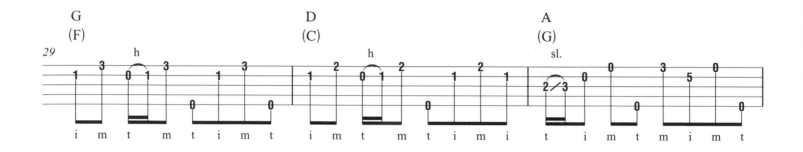

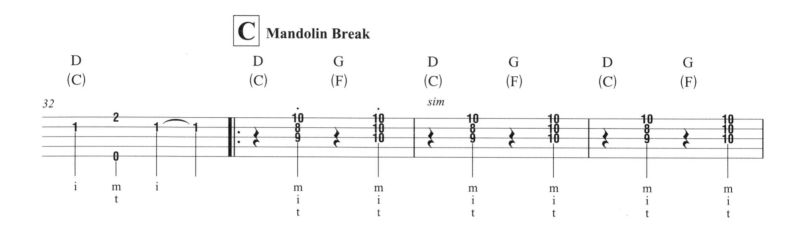

**C** Mandolin Break

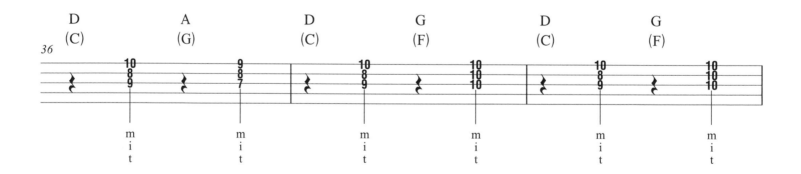

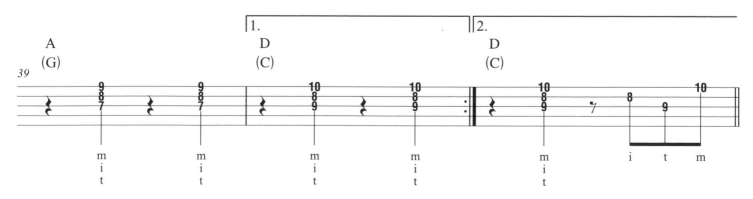

**D**

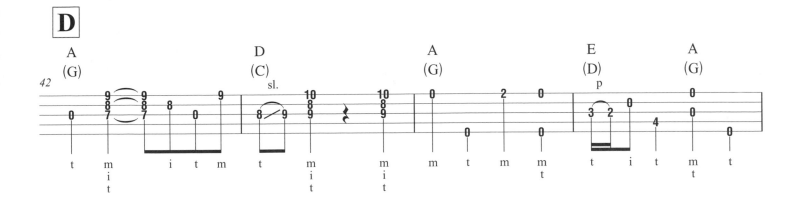

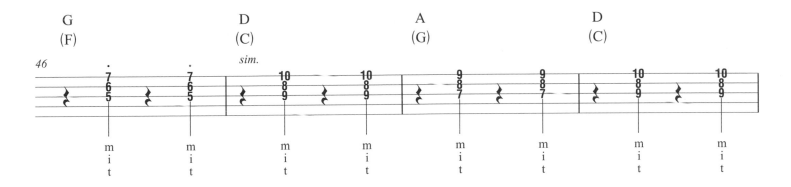

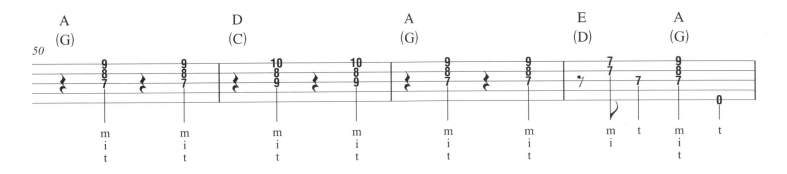

Capo VII

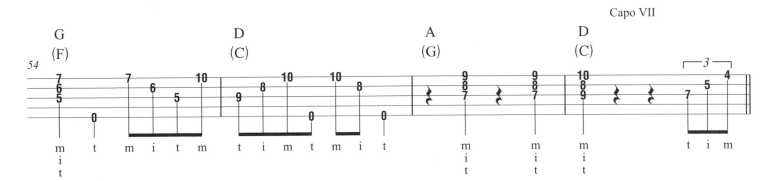

**E** Banjo Break

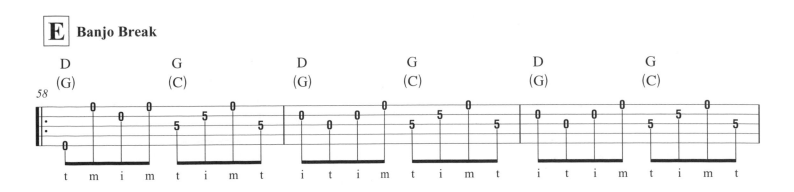

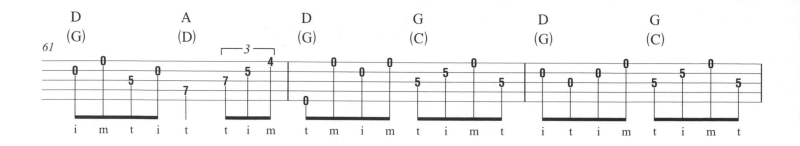

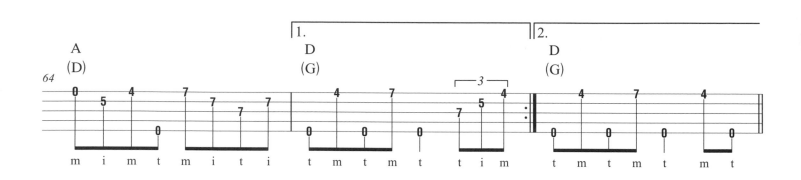

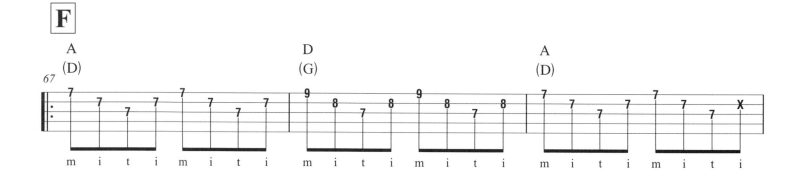

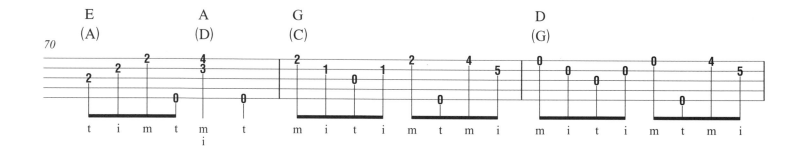

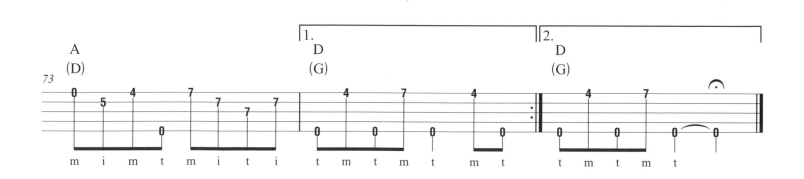

# Little Maggie

**Traditional**

G tuning:
(5th-1st) G-D-G-B-D

**Key of B**
Capo IV

**A** Banjo Break

Moderately ♩ = 108

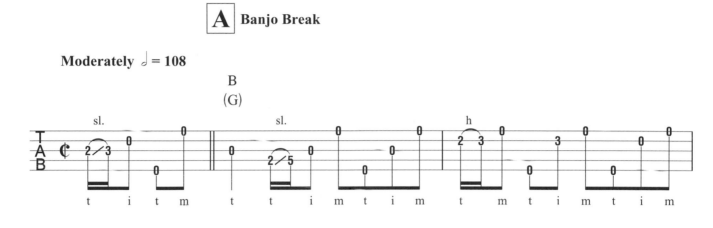

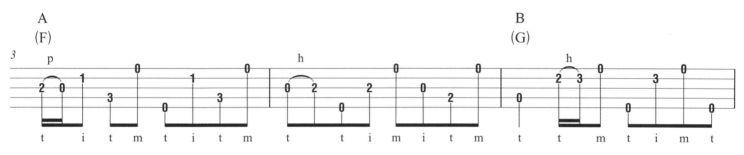

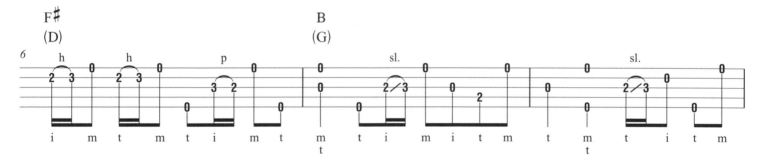

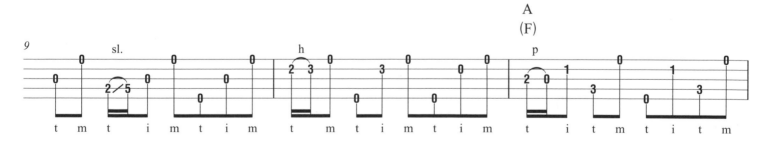

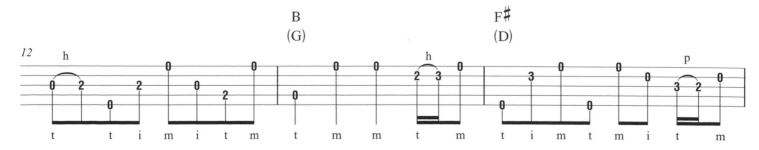

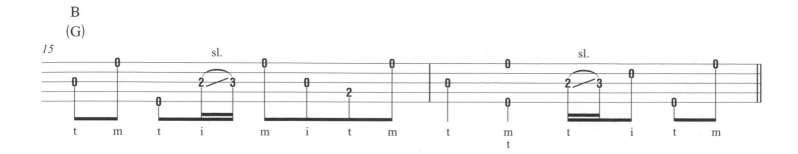

## B

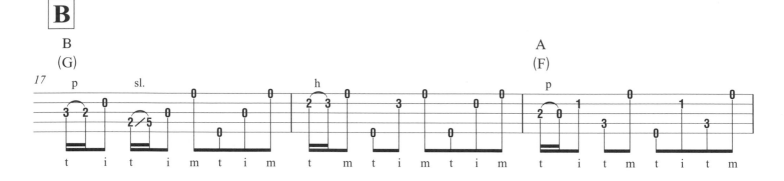

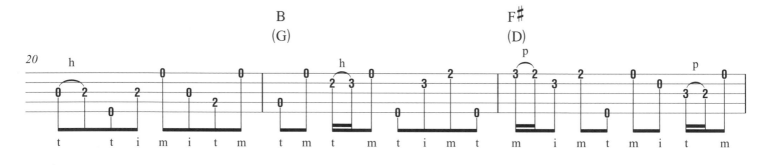

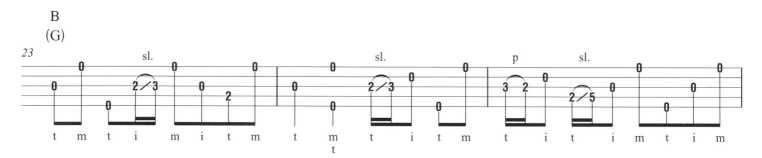

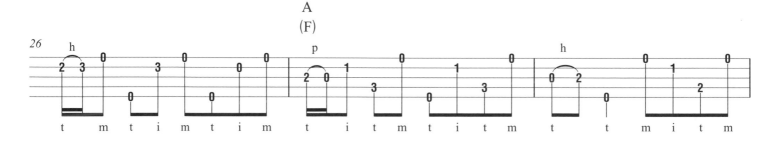

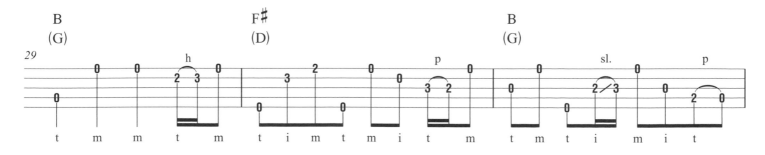

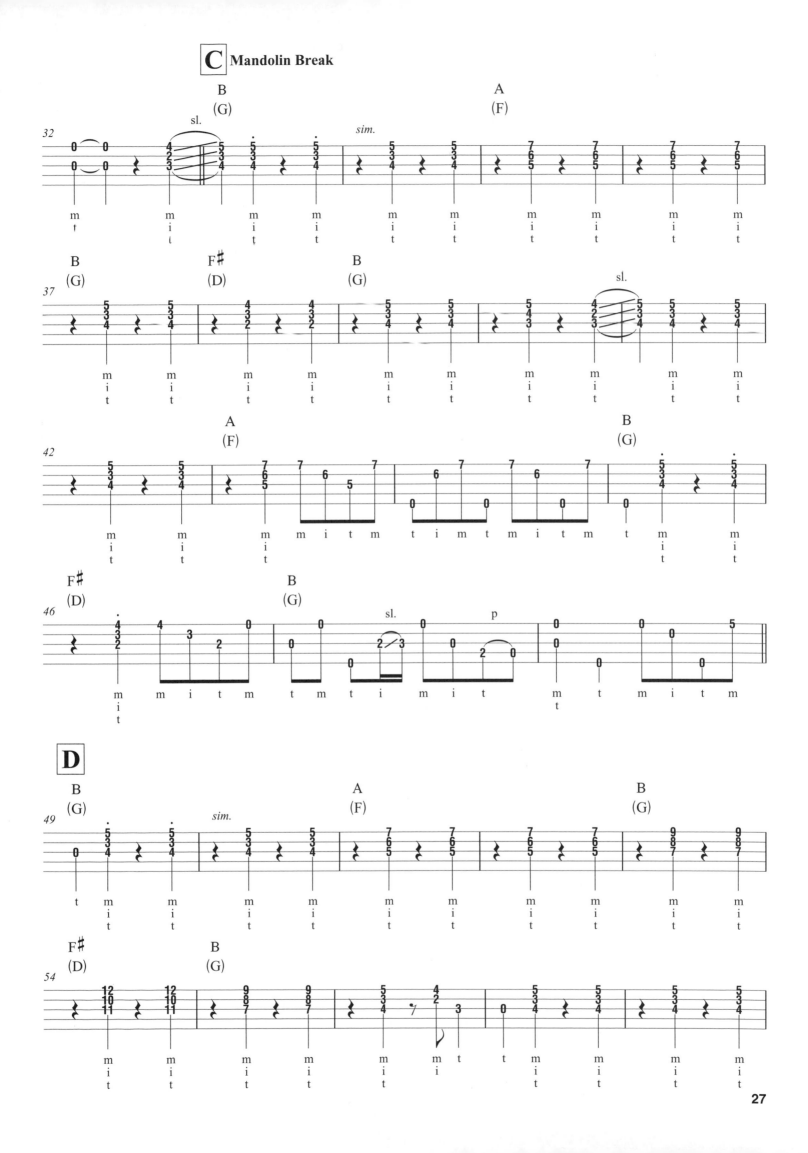

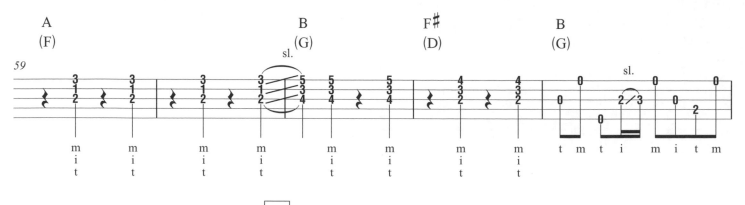

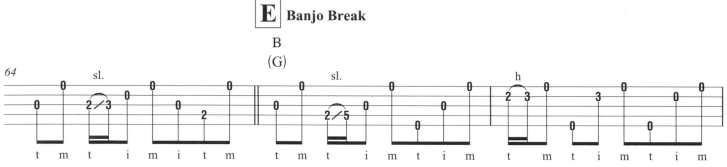

## E Banjo Break

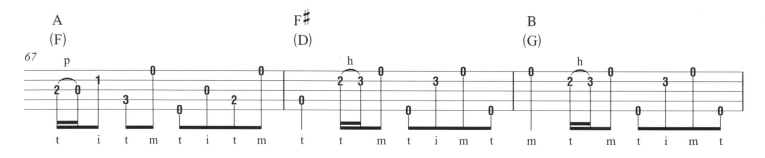

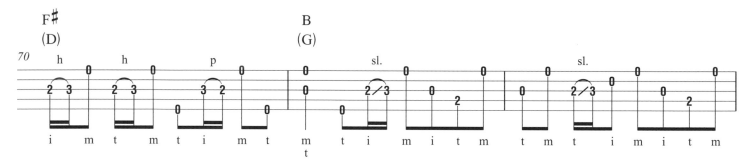

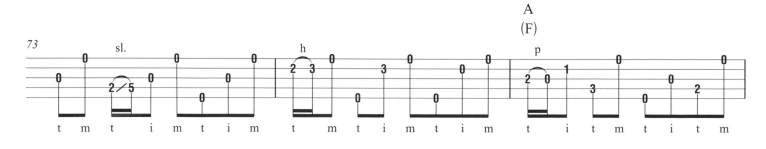

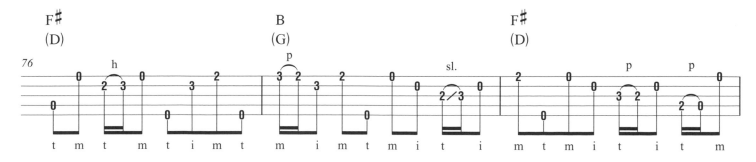

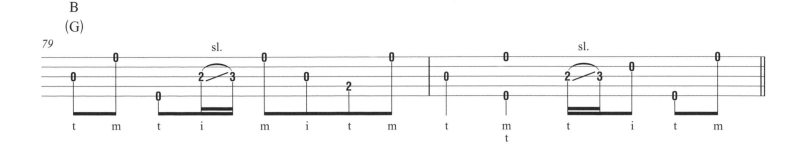

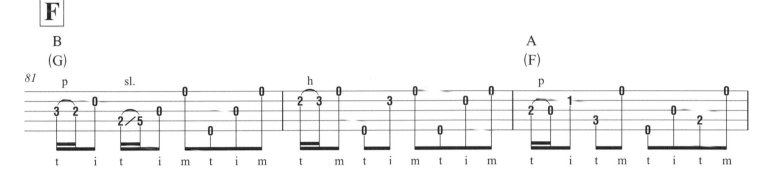

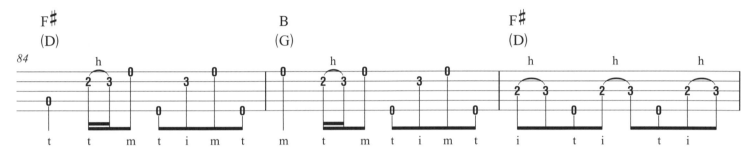

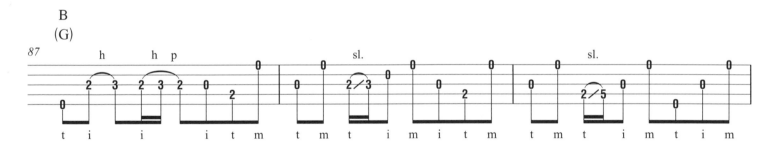

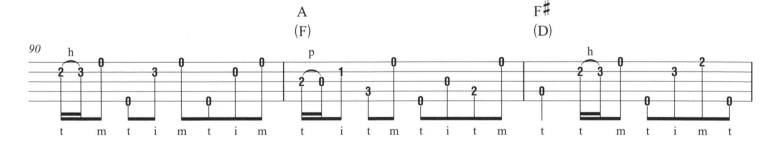

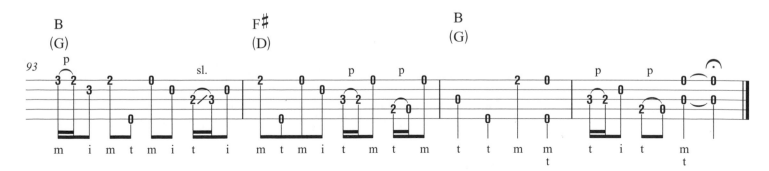

# Over the Waterfall

**Traditional Fiddle Tune**

G tuning:
(5th-1st) G-D-G-B-D

**Key of D**
Capo VII

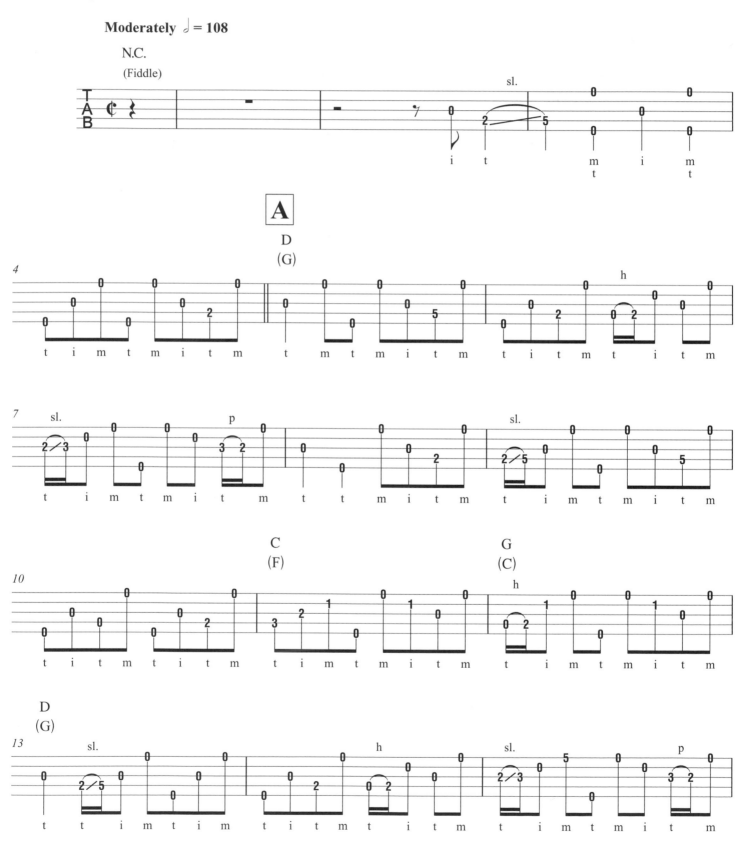

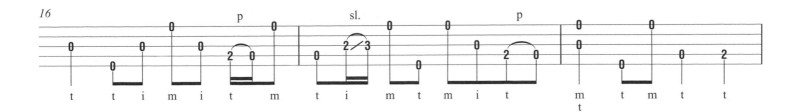

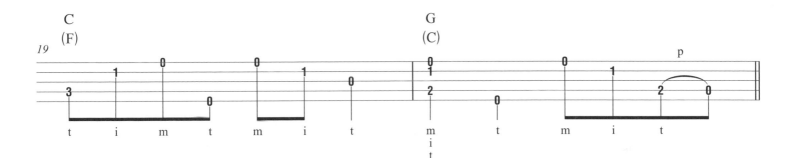

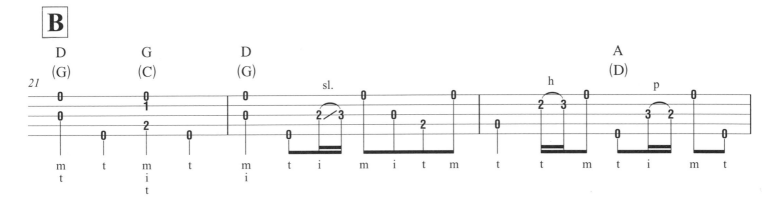

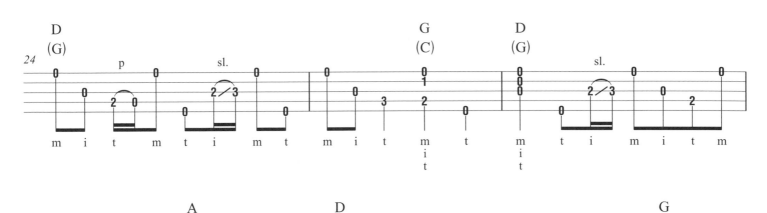

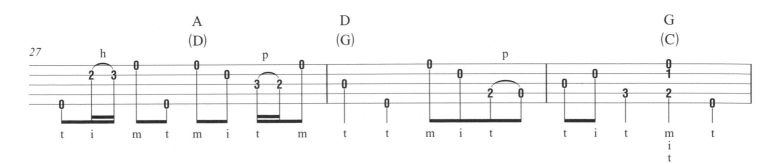

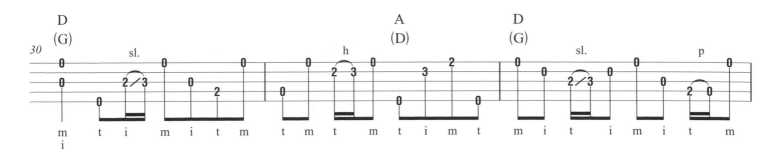

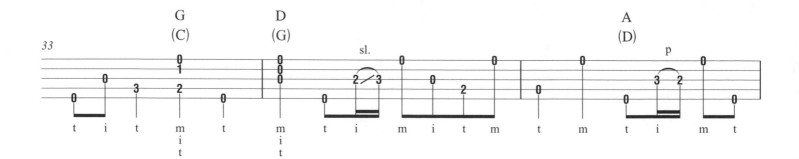

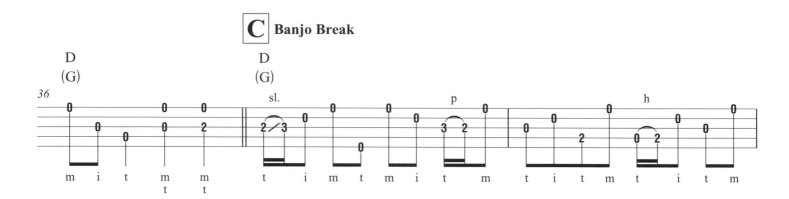

**C** Banjo Break

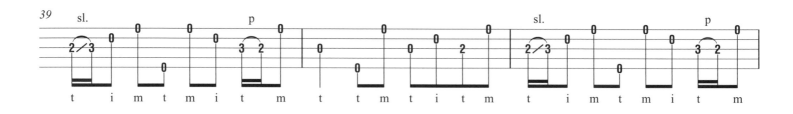

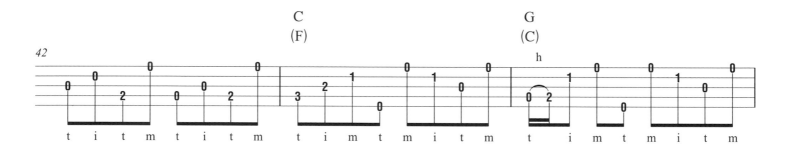

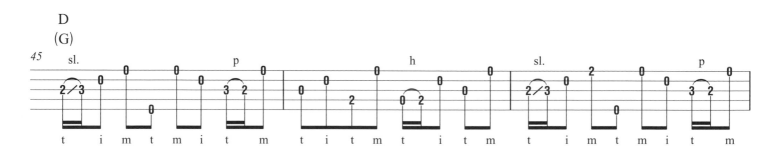

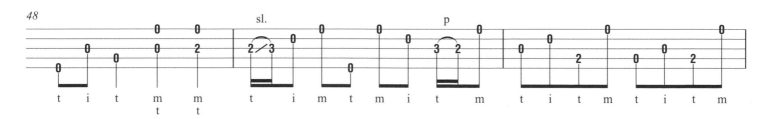

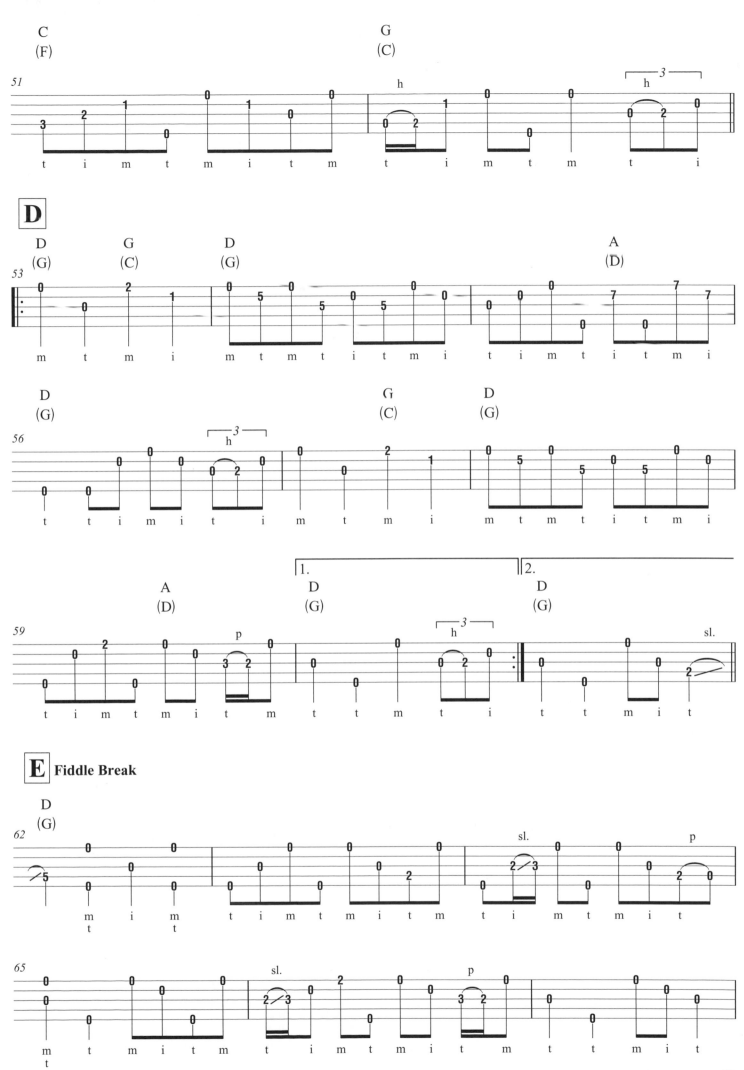

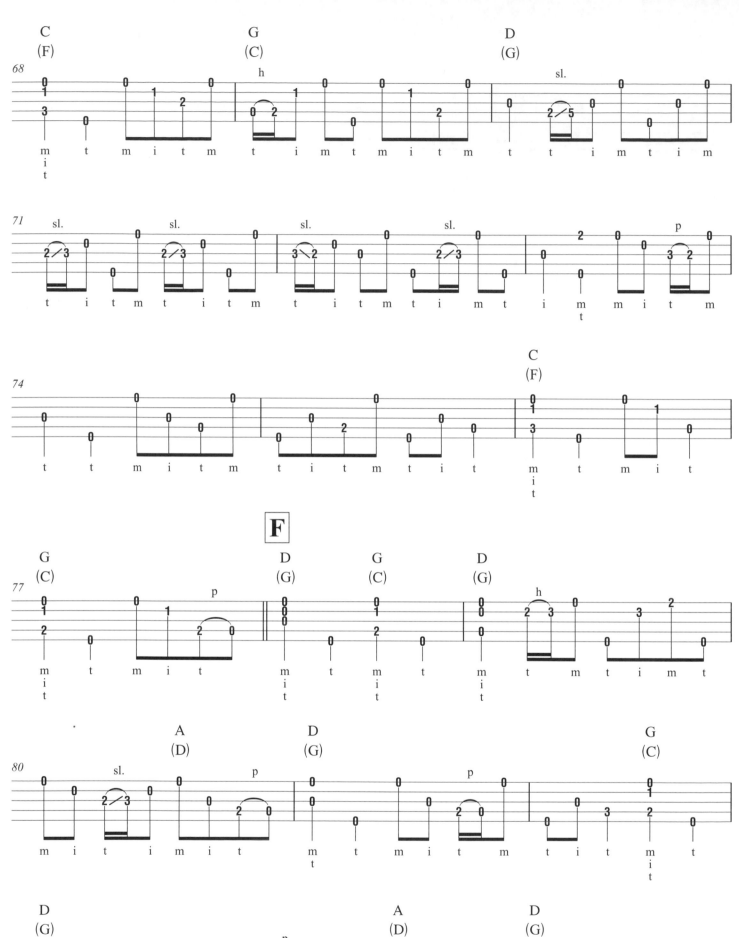

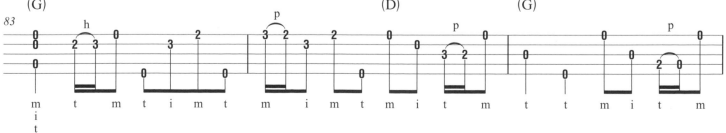

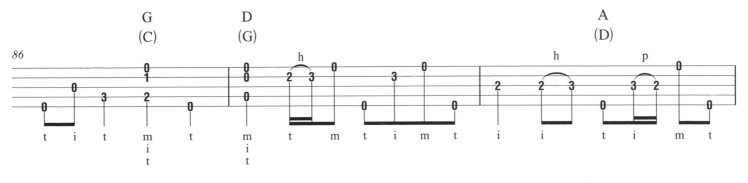

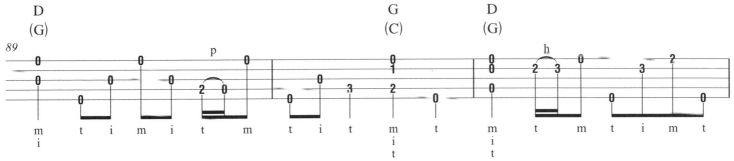

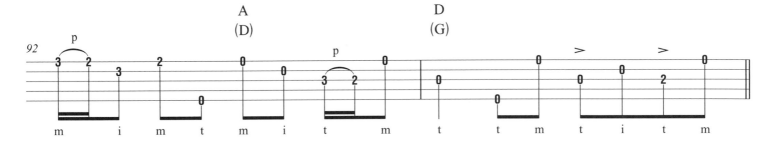

**G** Banjo Break

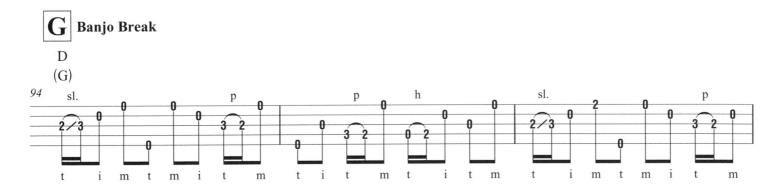

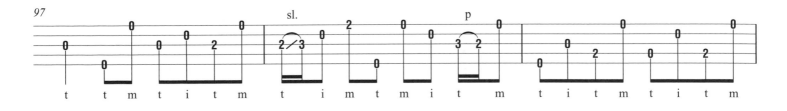

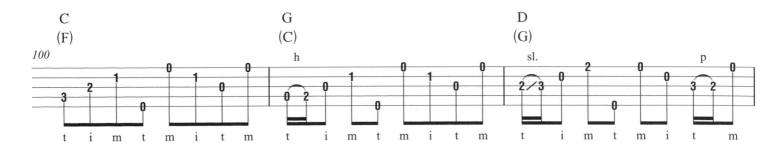

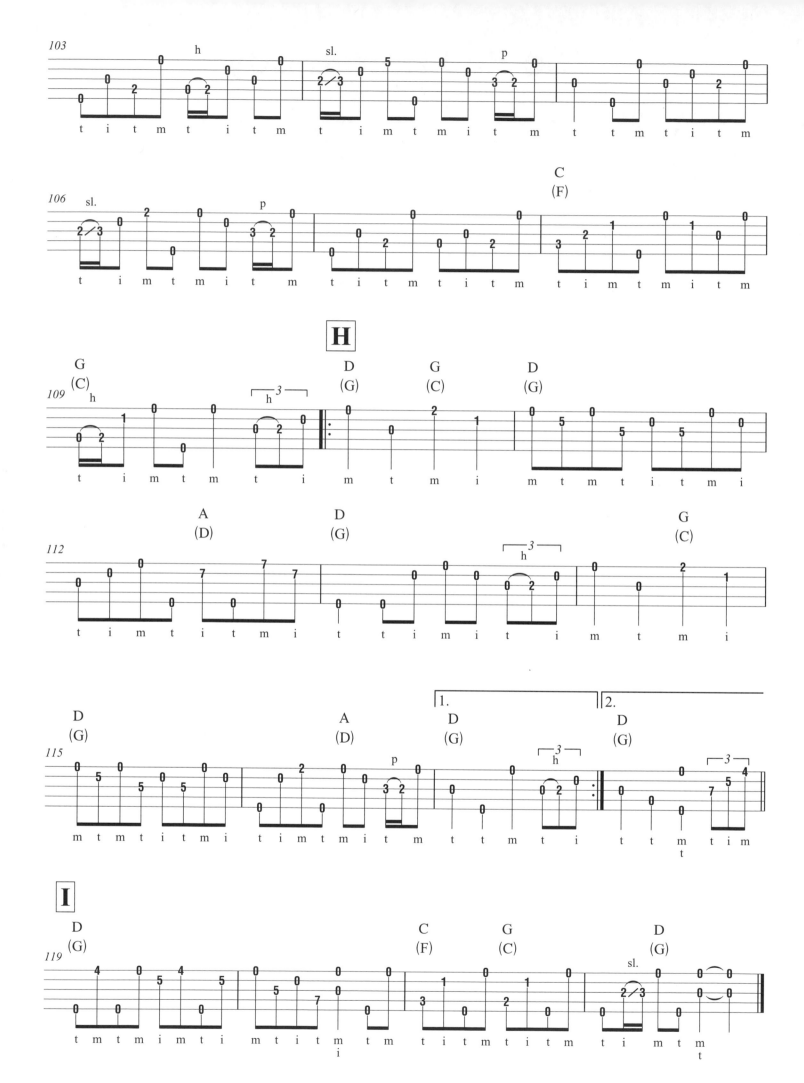

# The Red Haired Boy

**Old Time Fiddle Tune**

G tuning:
(5th-1st) G-D-G-B-D

**Key of A**
Capo II

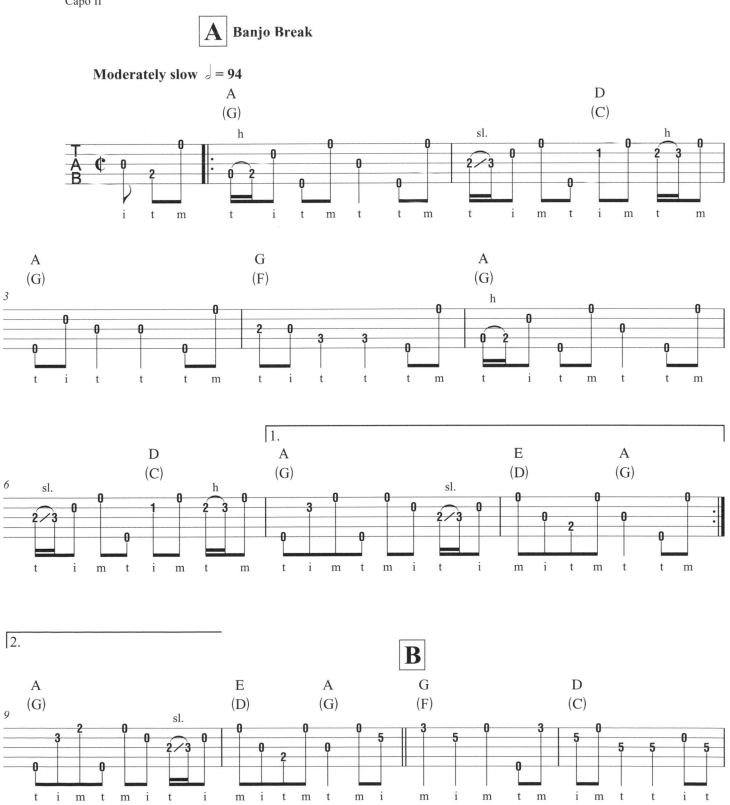

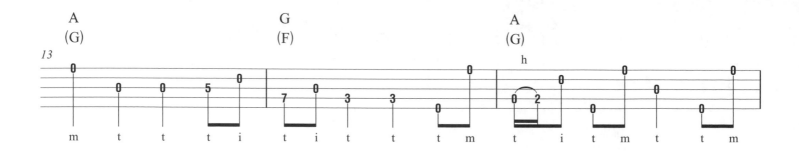

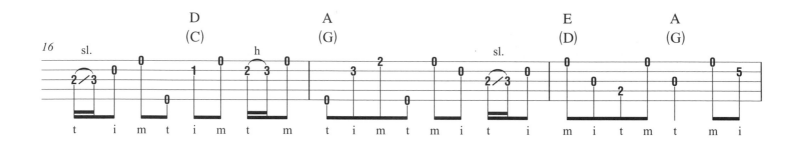

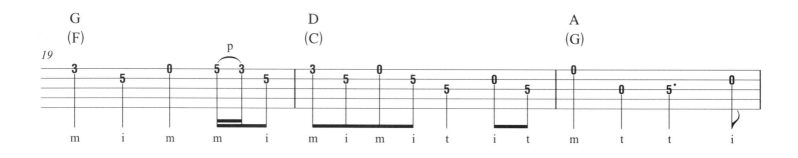

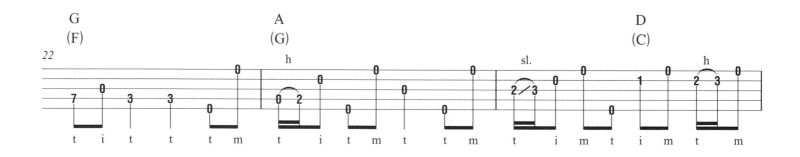

C | Mandolin Break

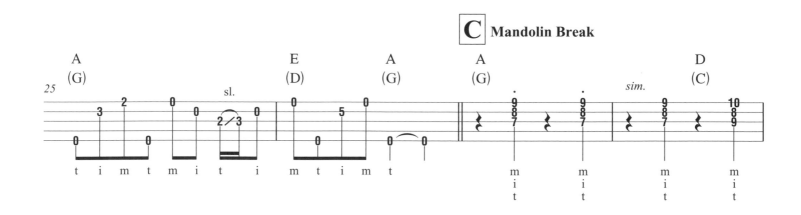

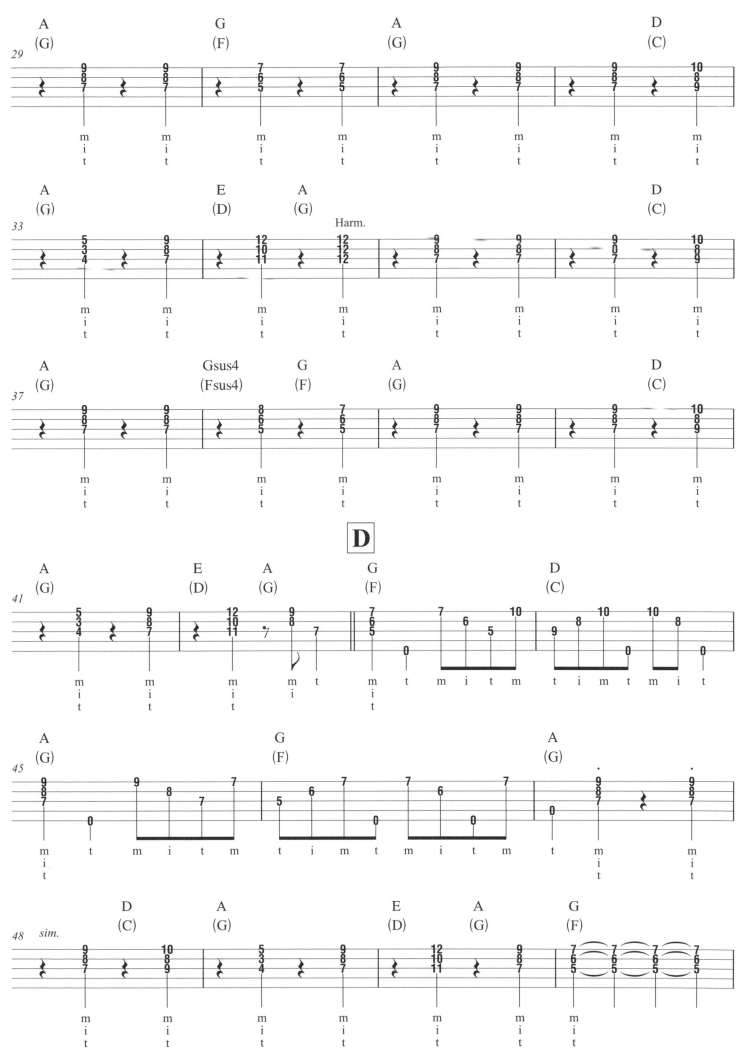

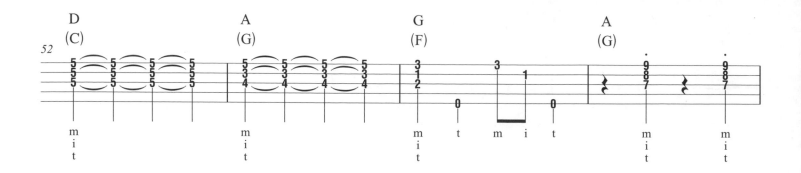

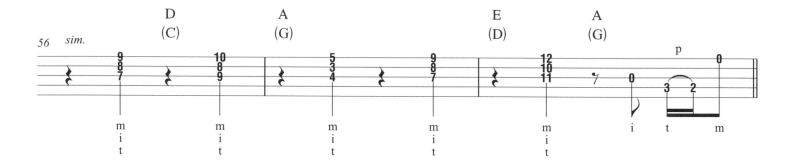

**E** Banjo Break

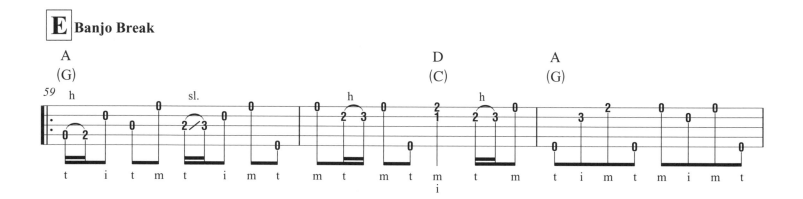

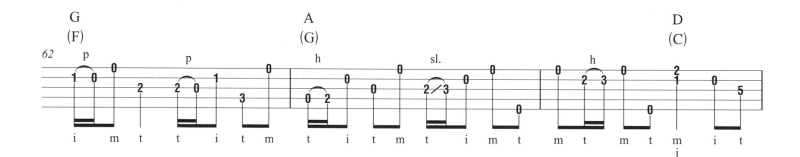

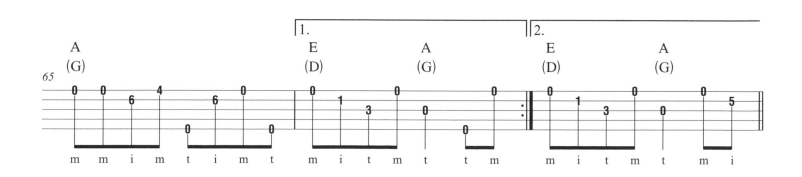

**F**

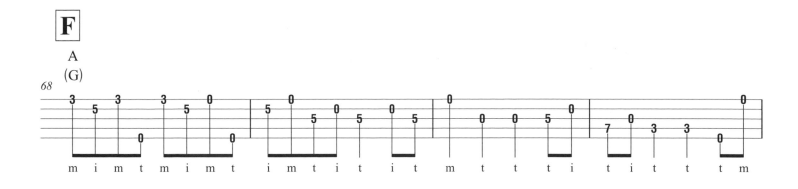

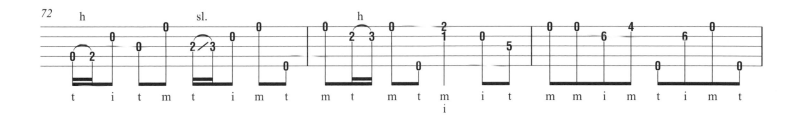

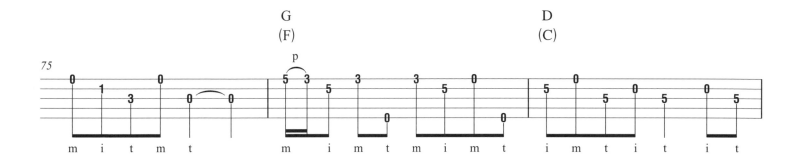

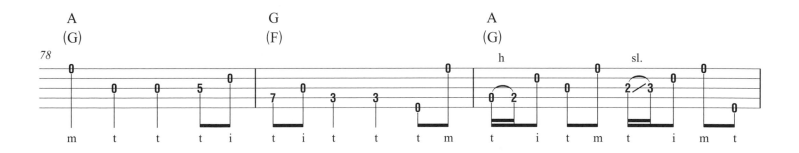

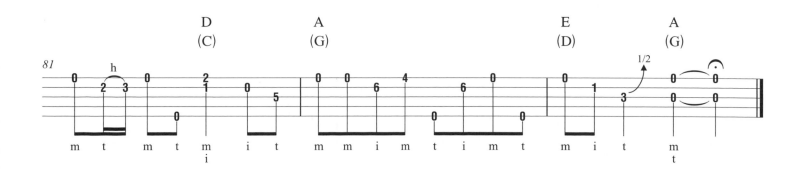

# Soldier's Joy

**Traditional**

G tuning:
(5th-1st) G-D-G-B-D

**Key of D**
Capo VII

 **Banjo Break**

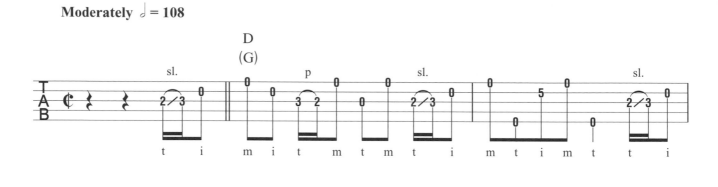

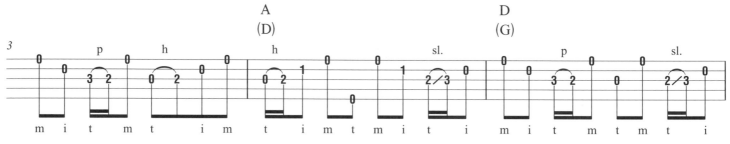

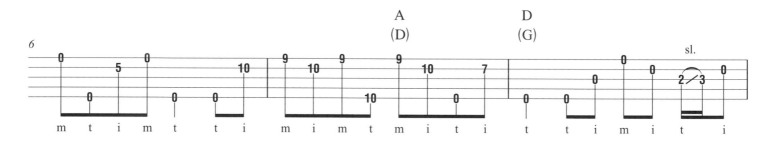

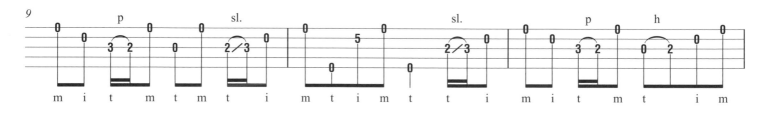

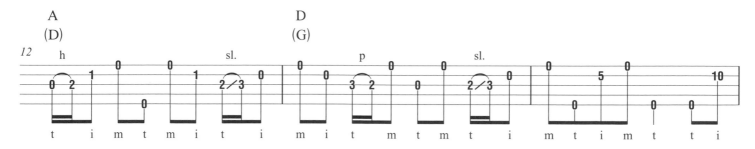

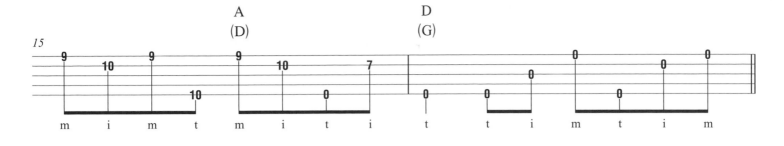

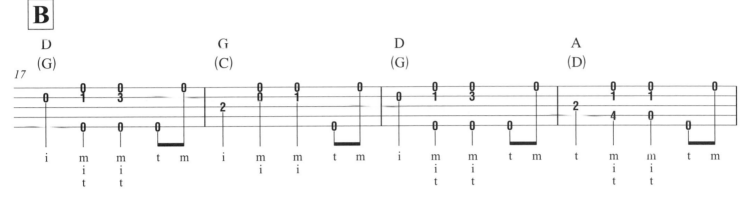

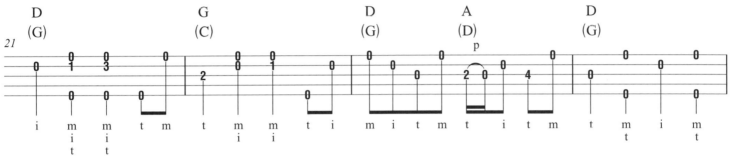

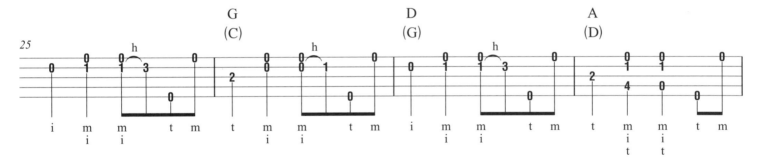

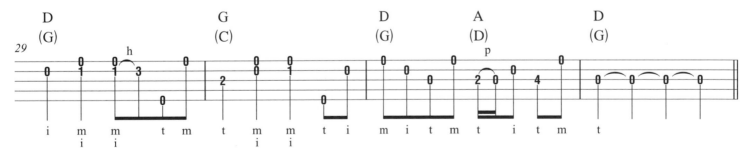

**C** Mandolin Break

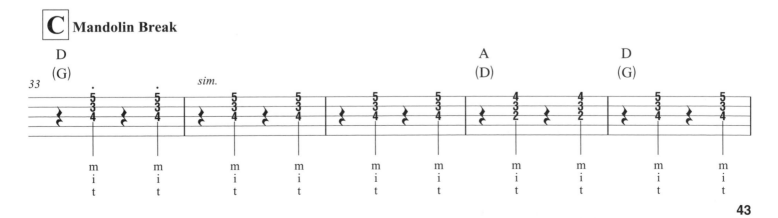

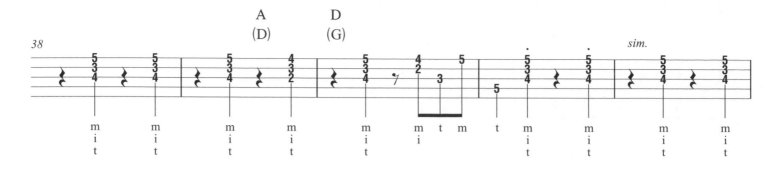

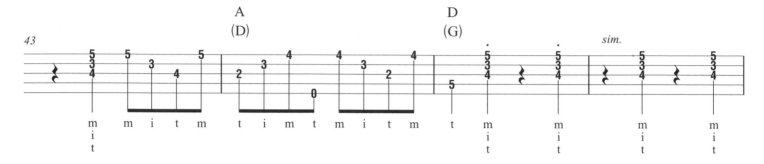

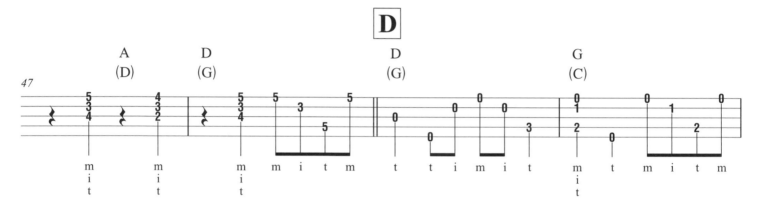

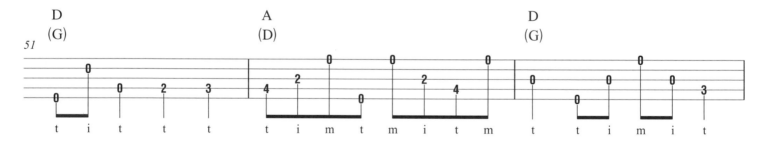

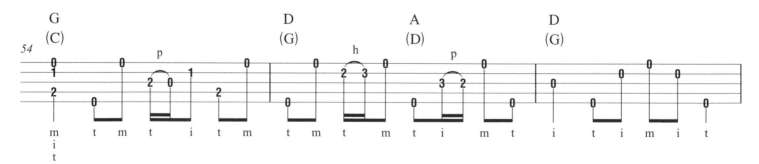

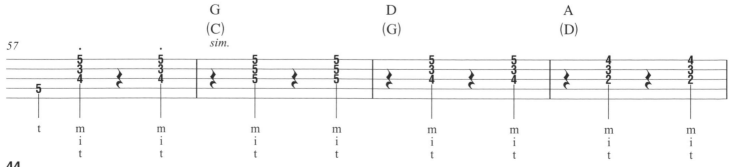

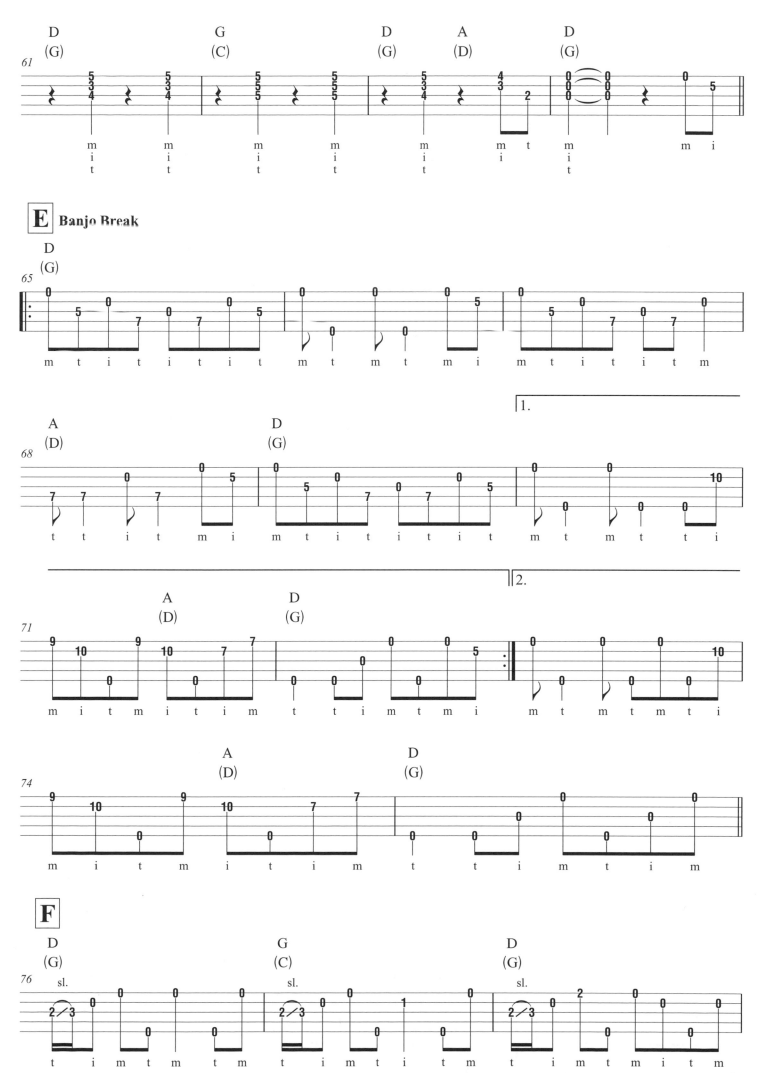

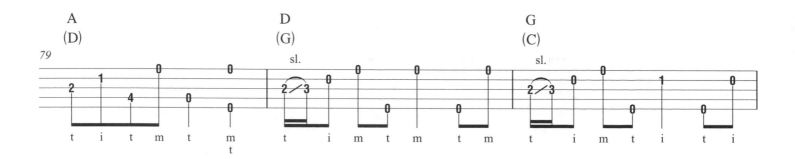

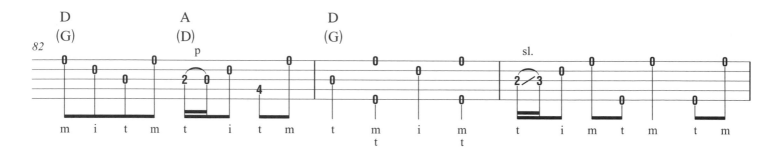

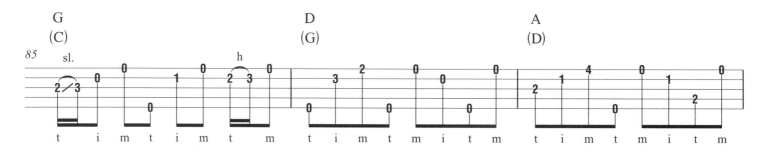

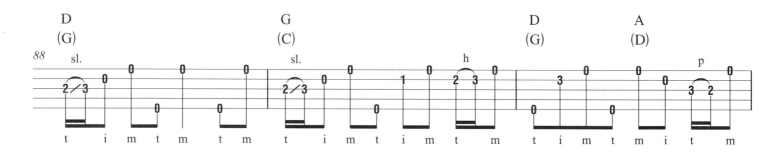

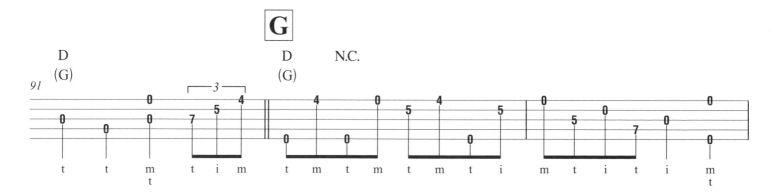

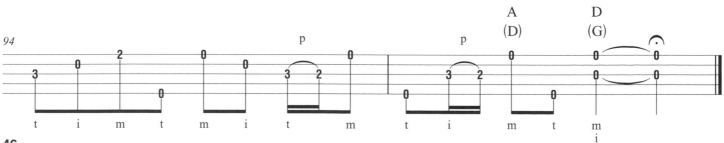

# BANJO NOTATION LEGEND

**TABLATURE** graphically represents the banjo fingerboard. Each horizontal line represents a string, and each number represents a fret.

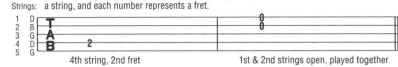

4th string, 2nd fret          1st & 2nd strings open, played together

**TIME SIGNATURE:**
The upper number indicates the number of beats per measure, the lower number indicates that a quarter note gets one beat.

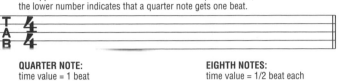

**CUT TIME:**
Each note's time value should be cut in half. As a result, the music will be played twice as fast as it is written.

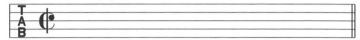

**QUARTER NOTE:**
time value = 1 beat

**EIGHTH NOTES:**
time value = 1/2 beat each

single          in series

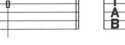

**SIXTEENTH NOTES:**
time value = 1/4 beat each

single          in series

**DOTTED QUARTER NOTE:**
time value = 1 1/2 beat

**TIE:** Pick the 1st note only, then let it sustain for the combined time value.

**TRIPLET:** Three notes played in the same time normally occupied by two notes of the same time value.

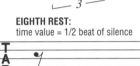

**GRACE NOTE:** A quickly played note with no time value of its own. The grace note and the note following it only occupy the time value of the second note.

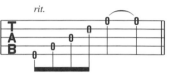

**RITARD:** A gradual slowing of the tempo or speed of the song.

**QUARTER REST:**
time value = 1 beat of silence

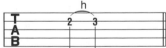

**EIGHTH REST:**
time value = 1/2 beat of silence

**HALF REST:**
time value = 2 beats of silence

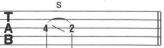

**WHOLE REST:**
time value = 4 beats of silence

**ENDINGS:** When a repeated section has a first and second ending, play the first ending only the first time and play the second ending only the second time.

**REPEAT SIGNS:** Play the music between the repeat signs two times.

**D.S. AL CODA:**
Play through the music until you complete the measure labeled *"D.S. al Coda,"* then go back to the sign (𝄋).
Then play until you complete the measure labeled *"To Coda ⊕,"* then skip to the section labeled *" ⊕ Coda."*

𝄋                    *To Coda* ⊕                    *D.S. al Coda*                    ⊕ *Coda*

**HAMMER-ON:** Strike the first (lower) note with one finger, then sound the higher note (on the same string) with another finger by fretting it without picking.

**PULL-OFF:** Place both fingers on the notes to be sounded. Strike the first note and without picking, pull the finger off to sound the second (lower) note.

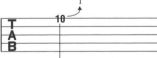

**SLIDE UP:** Strike the first note and then slide the same fret-hand finger up to the second note. The second note is not struck.

**SLIDE DOWN:** Strike the first note and then slide the same fret-hand finger down to the second note. The second note is not struck.

**HALF-STEP CHOKE:** Strike the note and bend the string up 1/2 step.

**WHOLE-STEP CHOKE:** Strike the note and bend the string up one step.

**NATURAL HARMONIC:** Strike the note while the fret-hand lightly touches the string directly over the fret indicated.

**BRUSH:** Play the notes of the chord indicated by quickly rolling them from bottom to top.

## Scruggs/Keith Tuners:

**HALF-TWIST UP:** Strike the note, twist tuner up 1/2 step, and continue playing.

**HALF-TWIST DOWN:** Strike the note, twist tuner down 1/2 step, and continue playing.

**WHOLE-TWIST UP:** Strike the note, twist tuner up one step, and continue playing.

**WHOLE-TWIST DOWN:** Strike the note, twist tuner down one step, and continue playing.

## Right Hand Fingerings

t = thumb          i = index finger          m = middle finger

# Hal Leonard Banjo Play-Along Series

## HAL•LEONARD® BANJO PLAY-ALONG

AUDIO ACCESS INCLUDED

INCLUDES TAB

*The Banjo Play-Along Series will help you play your favorite songs quickly and easily with incredible backing tracks to help you sound like a bona fide pro! Just follow the banjo tab, listen to the demo track on the CD or online audio to hear how the banjo should sound, and then play along with the separate backing tracks. The CD is playable on any CD player and also is enhanced so Mac and PC users can adjust the recording to any tempo without changing the pitch! Books with online audio also include **PLAYBACK+** options such as looping and tempo adjustments. Each Banjo Play-Along pack features eight cream of the crop songs.*

## 1. BLUEGRASS
Ashland Breakdown • Deputy Dalton • Dixie Breakdown • Hickory Hollow • I Wish You Knew • I Wonder Where You Are Tonight • Love and Wealth • Salt Creek.
00102585 Book/CD Pack.........................$14.99

## 2. COUNTRY
East Bound and Down • Flowers on the Wall • Gentle on My Mind • Highway 40 Blues • If You've Got the Money (I've Got the Time) • Just Because • Take It Easy • You Are My Sunshine.
00105278 Book/CD Pack.........................$14.99

## 3. FOLK/ROCK HITS
Ain't It Enough • The Cave • Forget the Flowers • Ho Hey • Little Lion Man • Live and Die • Switzerland • Wagon Wheel.
00119867 Book/CD Pack.........................$14.99

## 4. OLD-TIME CHRISTMAS
Away in a Manger • Hark! the Herald Angels Sing • Jingle Bells • Joy to the World • O Holy Night • O Little Town of Bethlehem • Silent Night • We Wish You a Merry Christmas.
00119889 Book/CD Pack.........................$14.99

## 5. PETE SEEGER
Blue Skies • Get up and Go • If I Had a Hammer (The Hammer Song) • Kisses Sweeter Than Wine • Mbube (Wimoweh) • Sailing Down My Golden River • Turn! Turn! Turn! (To Everything There Is a Season) • We Shall Overcome.
00129699 Book/CD Pack.........................$17.99

## 6. SONGS FOR BEGINNERS
Bill Cheatham • Black Mountain Rag • Cripple Creek • Grandfather's Clock • John Hardy • Nine Pound Hammer • Old Joe Clark • Will the Circle Be Unbroken.
00139751 Book/CD Pack.........................$14.99

## 7. BLUEGRASS GOSPEL
Cryin' Holy unto the Lord • How Great Thou Art • I Saw the Light • I'll Fly Away • I'll Have a New Life • Man in the Middle • Turn Your Radio On • Wicked Path of Sin.
00147594 Book/Online Audio ...............$14.99

## 8. CELTIC BLUEGRASS
Billy in the Low Ground • Cluck Old Hen • Devil's Dream • Fisher's Hornpipe • Little Maggie • Over the Waterfall • The Red Haired Boy • Soldier's Joy.
00160077 Book/Online Audio ...............$14.99

## HAL•LEONARD®
www.halleonard.com

1216